The Business
Security
Handbook

OTHER BOOKS BY GARY MURRAY

ENEMIES OF THE STATE: An exposé of the
Private Detective Industry and the Security Services

AN INTRODUCTION TO JUDO: An examination
of a Japanese Martial Art

The Business
Security
Handbook

GARY MURRAY

SIMON & SCHUSTER

LONDON · SYDNEY · NEW YORK · TOKYO · SINGAPORE · TORONTO

First published in Great Britain by Simon & Schuster, 1996
A Viacom Company

Simon & Schuster Ltd
West Garden Place
Kendal Street
London
W2 2AQ

Simon & Schuster of Australia Pty Ltd
Sydney

A CIP catalogue record for this book is
available from the Britsh Library.

ISBN 0-684 81669-5

Typeset in Goudy Old Style
by Hewer Text Composition Services, Edinburgh
Printed and bound in Great Britain
by Butler and Tanner, Frome, Somerset

Contents

Introduction

The current erratic economic and business climate is such that company directors and business managers are engaged in a constant battle to run their businesses efficiently. Success and profitability are elusive goals sought after by everyone in business today but sadly the Bankruptcy Courts present a dismal picture, with thousands of liquidations each year. The only firms who seem to thrive in such times are solicitors, accountants and other legal and financial practices. These services are in great demand now, more than ever before in fact. While there are always purposes for which businesses must and should turn to such professionals, they are usually expensive and can be damaging to the profit margin of a struggling firm. Hopefully this book will remind business managers of the areas where preventative measures can be taken, in order to avoid costly cures.

Already in 1995 major scandals exposing breaches of security and criminal activity within some of Britain's largest companies have appeared in the media. The first revelation to hit the headlines this year highlighted grave security breaches at Sun Alliance, the country's biggest insurance company. In January, insurance officials discovered that confidential information about policy holders had gone astray when secret documents – containing client's names and addresses, the value of their possessions, details of valuable items and security precautions – had been wrongly sent out from one of the broker centres. Security experts described the whole affair as a 'burglar's charter'. The papers – home contents schedules – were mistakenly sent to a private address in West London, instead of an independent broker acting for Sun Alliance. In addition, there was other commercially sensitive material relating to commissions paid by Sun Alliance to brokers which are added on to the premiums charged to policy holders. Fortunately, the recipient of the misdirected documents sent them on to the correct address, and alerted Sun Alliance's national broker centre in Oldham. Amazingly, more wrongly directed documents, all saturated with confidential customer and commercial information, continued to arrive at the West London address.

The thought of such sensitive information falling into the hands of *anyone* is too serious to contemplate, especially when the firm holding the data is earning £4.5 billion a year, of which £550 million comes from home contents policies. One would think that Sun Alliance could have afforded to engage a more secure system to protect customer information.

The following month an even more serious breach of security occurred within one of the country's oldest and most prestigious banking organisations: Barings, bankers to the Queen and the secret intelligence service (MI6), suddenly ceased trading when it was revealed that a member of staff had allegedly engaged in illegal practices, resulting in the collapse of the Baring empire. For several days, the media targeted a Singapore based employee, naming him as being responsible for all manner of irregularities. However, as the publicity mist cleared, there emerged a strong possibility that other senior officials had been involved in a worldwide investment 'scam' for over a year. Investigations are now underway, and it will probably take several months to uncover the truth of this affair.

These two examples show that faulty systems and staff misconduct can seriously undermine business operations. However, the running of a successful business can be inhibited by other factors, including cash-flow, missing debtors and industrial espionage, all of which contribute to a decline in general efficiency and progress. These and many other problems result in a steady flow of bankruptcies every month, with some firms having to sell out to predators, waiting to take advantage of unstable situations.

This manual will assist corporations, medium and small-scale organisations to police their own affairs. Hopefully, even the 'one-man band' will be able to benefit from this book. The author an experienced criminal-security investigator and former counter intelligence agent, has for many years applied his expertise to the business fraternity. His clients include banks, multi-national firms, credit card organisations, finance houses and numerous other industrial and commercial conglomerates who have utilised his unique knowledge to safeguard their interests.

1   Financial Investigations

If a company or sole trader is to survive and progress in business there are a number of essential courses of action that should be adopted with regard to the granting of credit facilities, settlement of invoices and dealing with debtors. By creating an in-house system and resisting the temptation to enlist the sometimes expensive services of lawyers or accountants, cash-flow can be improved and problems relating to delinquent customers and outstanding accounts controlled.

Application for Credit Facilities

There are two types of application for credit facilities: those from companies and those from individuals. Depending on the facilities required by such applicants the following investigations should be activated before services or goods are supplied on a credit basis. It could well be that the supplier is not in the habit of providing services or goods without payment in advance, in which case investigations into a potential customer's status will not be required.

Company Applications

Let us imagine that ABC Technical Service Limited has applied to purchase services or goods on a continuing basis, the result of which is that they will be required to settle monthly accounts to the tune of several hundreds or even thousands of pounds. The supplier should request the applicant to complete a detailed credit application proforma. In particular, the following information should be requested:

- Full title of company and registration number
- Names and home addresses of all directors
- Number of years in business
- Name and address of the company accountants
- Date of last annual return and audited accounts
- Registered and trading address of the company bankers
- Three trade references from satisfied suppliers
- Details of any court judgements involving outstanding financial disputes along with reasons for such disputes

Once the above information has been received and analysed the supplier should then be in a position to decide if further enquiries are necessary. The amount of anticipated business and money involved could well be substantial enough to justify extensive enquiries. In particular, the supplier should be wary of the following warning signs:

(a) The applicant is a recently formed limited company, consequently it has not traded long enough to get established in business. In such cases it is more than likely that audited accounts have not yet been registered with Companies House, which means the supplier will not have access to useful information from these sources.

(b) If the applicants have failed to provide a company registration number, this could mean that the firm named is not in fact a corporate organisation as such and therefore does not have to file annual accounts. Once again, in-depth research will not be possible.

(c) If it is admitted on the initial application for credit that County Court judgements have been awarded against the applicant, the supplier should query the circumstances of such judgements before granting credit facilities.

It is important to note that before any decision is made the supplier should arrange to acquire trade references and a copy of the applicant's company file, which is legally available to the public.

Trade references   Suitably prepared letters should be dispatched to the three trade referees supplied on the application form. While generally this is a useful form of collecting evidence of an applicant's business potential, it should always be remembered that in cases of planned deception it is not uncommon for trade references to be bogus.

Company file   By either applying direct to Companies House or utilising the sources of an agency, the official file relating to the applicant firm can be obtained. If applying direct to Companies House, use the addresses and phone numbers on page 160.

Once the company file is obtained the supplier (or agent) will have access to details of the applicant's financial state, that is assuming annual accounts have been filed as required by law. Copies of such accounts are presented in the examples section of this book. If annual accounts have not been filed up to date, then suppliers should be wary. Generally speaking, the company file is a good source of 'intelligence' for the supplier. It should be carefully analysed, along with trade references, by someone who is familiar with accounts.

One additional source of information is **The Registry of County Court Judgements** (for address see page 162). This organisation holds records of County Court debt-judgements awarded against individuals, traders or corporate firms. Such information is not normally contained on the company file unless a liquidation or winding-up has occurred. The above named registry can be accessed by the supplier direct or via one of the many agents operating throughout the country.

One of the most expedient and economical methods of investigating any application for credit is to subscribe to one of the major credit referencing agencies, such as CCN or 1 Equifax Europe (UK) Ltd., addresses on page 163. These organisations are well versed in checking out applications for credit and if there are any financial skeletons in the cupboard, they should find them. Businesses across the country are now using these agencies, rather than undertaking direct searches.

However, suppliers can now activate their requests for information via 'on-line' computer services and retrieve data within minutes, if they are equipped with the appropriate hardware. This on-line accessing is a very convenient and cost-effective method of checking creditworthiness.

On-line computer services   Although on-line accessing can be a very efficient method of carrying out credit checks, it requires a certain amount of skill and understanding in computer operations. Fortunately, all major services have manuals of instruction so to get a search up and running is not too difficult. A typical business search will involve typing into the computer terminal a code which relates to the specific type of information required. For example:

Product	Information Screen Code	Description
Registered Name & Address	1	This screen shows basic information available from Companies House. The address is the registered address which may not always be the same as the trading address. Telephone and fax numbers will be shown if available.
Documents Filed	2	This screen shows the latest dates of filing of key documents at Companies House.
Business Activity	3	This screen describes the activities of the company as indicated in the latest annual director's report. The activities are classified using the Standard Industrial Classification (1980).

Profit & Loss A/C	4	Details of up to 3 years of profit and loss account are shown. Smaller companies are not required to disclose the same amount of detail, e.g. medium-sized companies may omit turnover, small companies need not file a P & L statement.
Balance Sheet	5	Details of up to 3 years of the balance sheet are shown.
Details of Assets	6	A breakdown of up to 3 years of a company's assets and liabilities are shown.
Other Financial Information	7	This screen shows miscellaneous information extracted from the annual report and accounts, e.g. auditors, bankers and number of employees.
Holding/Subsidiaries	8	This screen shows the parent of the company being viewed and/or any subsidiary companies. There may be several pages if the selected company is part of a large group.
Directors	9	This screen shows the Directors and Company Secretary.
Profitability Ratios/ Trends	10	The ratios shown here are calculated from information

provided in the profit and loss account, with trends showing the actual and percentage changes year-on-year based on up to 3 years' accounts.

Financial Ratios/ Trends	11	The ratios shown here are calculated from information provided in the balance sheet, with trends showing the actual and percentage changes year-on-year based on up to 3 years' accounts.
Changes of Name	12	This screen shows any change of name which the company has undergone in the past 20 years.
Profile of Company	13	This is a single screen of data giving an overview of the financial performance of a company. Also shown are employee numbers, main director, ownership details and business activity.
Full Data on Company	14	Screens 1–12 are scrolled together so that you can either print all the information off at once or download the information to a file.
Ownership Structure	15	This shows the hierarchical structure of holding and subsidiary companies and the relationship between them.

If this operation is not preferred or possible then to pass the job to an established credit reference agency is probably the next best thing. For details of firms providing such services, refer to *nation-wide investigation organisations section* at the rear of this book.

Bank references The discreet and at at times secretive world of banking can mystify the average person with its jargon, especially in relation to references. The following information gleaned from various sources should serve as a useful guide to interpreting bank references:

Bank wording	Meaning
1. Undoubted.	1. Undoubted.
2. Considered good for your figure and purpose.	2. Good.
3. Respectable and considered trustworthy for your figure and purpose.	3. Not quite as good as 2 but still reasonably safe.
4. Respectable and trustworthy and we do not believe he would enter into a commitment he could not see his way to fulfil.	4. Honest but might be over stretched – caution.
5. Respectable and trustworthy but the figure for which you enquire is larger than we are used to seeing.	5. Ditto.
6. We are unable to speak for your figure.	6. Don't touch applicant with a barge pole.

Review of Warning Signs

- Company recently formed
- Annual accounts and returns not up to date
- Doubtful reference from bankers or trade sources
- County Court judgements registered

- Winding-up Orders registered on file
- Trade referees operating from same address as the applicant
- Heavy mortgages and loans filed
- Substantial tax losses recorded
- Trading from a private address

Review of Healthy Signs

- Long established firm
- Accounts and returns always up to date
- Good bank reference and good trade references
- No County Court judgements or Winding-up Orders
- Minimal or no mortgages or other loans
- Regular profits
- Same directors during life of the company
- Trading from business premises

Checking an Individual's Creditworthiness

The method of investigating an individual's credit status is only slightly different from that of a limited company; in many ways it is easier. Once again the services of a reputable, cost-effective agency are recommended. However, there is nothing to stop a supplier carrying out direct research.

On-line computer access is again the most expedient method of carrying out a check. Within minutes the supplier's investigator can retrieve details of confirmation of residency at the address supplied, via the electoral roll. If there are any debts registered at the applicant's address, then such information can also be made available, as will other financial loans registered in the customer's name. A typical database computer display will contain the following information.

21 Petersfield Crescent
Crosstown
Kelvington
KS10 9EZ

_____VOTERS_____

Rogers	Bryan S	89–92
Rogers	Paul H	
Stephens	David F	83–89
Stephens	Marie	
Stephens	John	87–89
		240389

____TRACE DETAILS HELD____

TR – Stephens DF   (New) 11/89
TR – Stephens MD   (New) 11/89

TR – *Trace Data held on file for new*
   addresses on Stephens

_____TELEPHONE DATA_____

Rogers BS (New)   (0613)459 5176
Stephens MD (Old) (0613)458 2177

____ FILE INFORMATION ____

CJ – Rogers BS	£625.	0791
CJ – Rogers BS	£425.	0891
CJ – Rogers PM	£1,265.	0591
CJ – Rogers BS t/a BSR Fabrications	£2,495.	0891
CJ – Rogers BS t/a BSR Fabrications	£810.	0192
VAR – Thomas W	£2,695.	0888
BKY – Thomas W	£0.	0892
ODI – Thomas W	£0.	0892

CJ – *County Court judgement registered against the above named individual*

BKY – *Bankruptcy against the named individual*

VAR – *Voluntary arrangement to clear outstanding debt*

ODI – *Bankruptcy order discharged*

SR – Stephens M D	Finance House	011091
SR – Rogers P M	Mail Order	270891
SR – Rogers B S	Bank	070992
SR – Rogers B S	Credit Card	030791

SR – *Searches made upon the above-named individual by the above-named companies*

FT – Rogers PM	£175 × 36	FIN080992
DF – Rogers BS	£500	FIN 230292
HP – Rogers	£120 × 48	RET 071089

FT – *Fixed term amount where the total repayable under the account is fixed at the outset and is repayable by regular monthly payments of equal amount. Amount in this case is 36 monthly repayments of £175.00*

DF – *Default notified by a subscriber in respect of a credit transaction, the amount outstanding at the date shown. Registered with us when the account is more than three months overdue.*

HP – *Hire Purchase account showing monthly instalments and date first opened.*

Database information is available in a variety of forms, including detailed information on the individual and his spouses. All banks, building societies and finance houses update this information regularly. For example, Mr Smith moves from 2 Park Avenue in January 1993 and leaves no forwarding address. However, he is compelled to inform his bankers, building societies and finance houses. In due course this information will be tied together at his old address, enabling you to trace his new address if required.

During the completion of an individual application for credit, which should ideally be carried out on the premises of the supplier, the customer should be requested to provide confirmation of his identity by way of a driving licence or other suitable document. Preferably a copy of whatever means is produced should be made and retained on the customer's file. The actual application completed by the customer (see examples section) should indicate a request for details of the customer's date of birth, which can then be checked against say his driving licence which does in fact contain a disguised birth date. For instance:

Driving licence number: *DOE 505061 J E 9LX*

To ascertain the holder's date of birth:
(1)   Take the centre section of the Driver Number, i.e. 50 50 61
(2)   The first digit + the last digit = the year, i.e. 51
(3)   The third and fourth digits in reverse order = the month, i.e. 05
(4)   The second and fifth digits together = the date, i.e. 06

Hence, the date of birth of John Doe is 6/05/51.

On more recently issued driving licences the subject's date of birth is printed in full and not encoded in this manner.

Employment   When vetting an individual it is important to direct attention to *employment*. It is essential that job, time so employed, and salary are confirmed. Where a customer presents himself as being *self-employed* then discreet research should be activated into the overall circumstances of the declared employment, paying particular attention to nature of work, age of business and current position with the Inland Revenue and

Customs & Excise regarding value added tax. As preferential creditors, these organisations will have a priority claim on the customer should he ever run into financial difficulties. In all cases of self-employment three trade references should be requested. It should be remembered that an individual trading on a self-employed basis has no legal obligation to file annual accounts with any organisation other than the Inland Revenue, who will not release copies for examination by any outside party. The supplier has to therefore rely solely on the customer to produce his accounts, which of course is not a legal requirement. In other words, the customer may well not be happy about providing intimate details of his trading figures to the supplier. It goes without saying that the supplier is under no obligation to provide credit facilities.

Warning Signs

1 Doubtful employment, i.e. self-employed and no accounts, not vat registered
2 Name not on electoral roll
3 Short time at address
4 County Court judgement registered either at current or previous address
5 Numerous financial commitments filed at address
5 County Court judgements registered against other named persons at address: this could indicate that applicant is adopting other names

Healthy Signs

1 Established long-term salaried employment
2 In case of self-employed, accounts up to date and vat registered
3 Name on electoral register
4 Long-time resident at address
5 No heavy commitments or judgements registered

Avoiding lawyers and accountants

For many years, businesses have employed the services of lawyers, accountants and other 'professionals' to an extent which is surprising given the sometimes exorbitant fees. However of late, questions and criticism of the legal fraternity have reached an unprecedented level, with thousands of complaints being submitted to The Solicitors' Complaints Bureau every year. A standard expression adopted by businessmen forced into employing lawyers speaks for itself: 'This is your lawyer speaking – and the meter is running.'

According to a recent survey by the *International Financial Law Review*, a good City of London lawyer will set you back £235–£350 per hour, these charges being the most expensive in the world. Why should City of London lawyers be so expensive and, more to the point, why do their clients let them get away with it? The answer is simple – the clients do not have the know-how or general expertise to deal with matters which on the surface appear to be complicated.

In many such cases, had common-sense precautions been implemented (say in connection with the credit checking of a new customer) then heavy legal charges could have been avoided. It is not uncommon for legal charges to exceed the amount of a debt that is being chased. When a successful court judgement is awarded against a debtor, it is usual for the court to award 'costs' against the debtor. However, the reality of many such situations is that the debtor is unable to repay either the debt or the costs, the result being the claimant is left in a worse financial situation than before he employed solicitors.

The good that emerges from such a situation is that the solicitors have invariably been paid up-front by the claimant. The message here is clear: business organisations, sole traders or partnerships can avoid such situations by adopting a 'do-it-yourself' policy of general business operations. Businessmen and women these days are well advised to adopt some of the know-how of detectives, lawyers and accountants.

To avoid the expensive pitfalls of litigation, certain strategies can be activated in-house. Many corporate organisations do in fact operate their own special investigation units whose daily task is checking and dealing with all aspects of financial control and litigation. Staff in these units are often ex-police officers, so it is not surprising they have a high degree of success. The following suggestions, advocated by Barclays Bank, serve as a useful guide to business credit management, which will hopefully result in minimal debts and keep the cash flowing.

1. **Establishing credit policy** Every company needs a clear credit policy. Make sure you have a credit and collections policy that everybody within your business, and your customers, are familiar with.

2. **Dealing with existing customers** Make sure that your customer is quickly made aware of any overdue invoices. You may wish to highlight this on their monthly statement, if appropriate. Re-check the creditworthiness of any customer who continues to withhold payment, and reduce your credit exposure. If there is a change of ownership of any business, reassess their creditworthiness.

3. **Dealing with new customers** Once you are satisfied with the creditworthiness of a new customer, ensure that payment terms are perfectly clear to them. Agree the terms in advance, as part of their contract. Make sure your customer understands that the price of goods/service is linked to the credit terms you have offered. Be specific about your payment terms. 'Our credit is 30 days' is not enough. It's better to specify, for example, 'Our credit terms are 30 days from the date our goods are dispatched.'

If you have time, and it is practical, visit new customers. Assess their operation and establish a relationship. Ask your customer for the name of the person who will be responsible for paying your invoices. Only when you are satisfied that you have taken all the necessary steps to ensure your customer is reliable, should you begin to supply services on the terms agreed.

4. **Having the right attitude** Don't be embarrassed about discussing money. Remember, if you've kept to your part of the deal, you have the right to be paid. Reflect this in your attitude: be polite, but firm. Be aware that you are competing for payment

with your customer's other suppliers. You are more likely to get paid on time if you establish a relationship with the person responsible for payment, and if your procedures are carefully designed and properly enforced.

5. **Keeping clear documentation**   One of the main reasons for late payment is incorrect documentation. Make sure you send accurate invoices/statements to the right person, at the right place, at the right time. Include the customer's order number. Send out invoices and statements quickly. If you don't do this, you can't expect to get paid on time. Make sure your credit terms and the actual date payment is due, are shown clearly on all relevant documentation – such as quotations, order acknowledgements, invoices and statements. Make sure that the address to which payments are to be made is also clearly stated. Ensure that any disputes or queries are dealt with immediately.

6. **Collecting your money on time**   Set a timetable for your collections routine and stick to it. Keep clear records including a record of all telephone conversations. Whether or not you have a computerised system, ensure that you can organise your 'Aged Debtors' list to show the largest debts first. Give priority to your largest accounts. Do so by means of a personal visit, by telephone or by fax.

Even small amounts should be chased by telephone whenever possible. If not, then use a programme of letters. Keep a follow-up system. If a promised cheque fails to arrive, chase it again straight away. Tell the person who ordered the goods in the first place about the delay. They may be unaware of the problem and may be able to accelerate payment.

Many small businesses feel at a disadvantage when they are particularly dependant on one or two main customers. This is, however, all the more reason to ensure that you follow a clear credit and collections policy. Use your customer's need for further supplies of your product as a way to obtain payment. In such circumstances, don't be afraid to discontinue supplies to non-payers.

7. **Chasers for unpaid bills**   There are various methods of operation one can adopt to encourage settlement of invoices. The formal, firm approach is not always good for customer

relations, especially when there are dozens of competitors that clients can turn to for a similar service. One system that has been in use for many years is **bill stickers**, which are described as comic chasers for unpaid bills. These are carefully designed labels which the creditor can stick onto invoices to clients. Many of these chasers are light-hearted, some a little more formal, but at the same time designed not to be over-aggressive in requesting settlement.

Creditors should avoid adopting a system *per se*, e.g. one sticker for one month and such like. Different clients react in various ways to demands for money: some will be amused at the approach, others just ignore it. Some debtors respond to threats of court and bailiffs, whilst others are best approached by a pleasant female who might be more difficult for the client to fob off. The golden rule is to start with the least forceful reminder, and get steadily stronger with each request. It is useful to use a wide variety of stickers: once a debtor has experienced one particular style of demand it will have less impact the next time around.

Finally, never delegate the use of account reminders to an office junior. A young, lively sense of humour may not always be in accord with some of the more valuable clients. On the other hand, one particular London firm went to the trouble of awarding an annual certificate for the worst payer of the year. Surprisingly, the client thought it was humorous.

The example stickers shown below are just a few of the many hundreds currently available in ready printed form at most stationers. Some creditors have been known to create their own design to accompany carefully worded comic overdue invoices.

Self-employed contractors

There is a type of business that appears to suffer more than partnerships or limited liability companies. The life of a self-employed contractor can be unstable in that work is spasmodic and certainly never guaranteed. And when it comes to collecting money owed by large firms, debt collecting can be an impossible task for the independent operator. For many large companies it is standard practice to pay bills at the last possible moment. This ensures the company balance sheet is kept high and bank charges are kept to a minimum. This is not good news for the self-employed Independent Trader, who invariably is struggling to make ends meet.

PLEASE NOTE that in order to save the trouble and expense incurred by collecting small Accounts, it is requested that this invoice be promptly paid

Payment of this **A/C** would be appreciated

THIS ACCOUNT BEING OVERDUE, A REMITTANCE BY RETURN WILL OBLIGE

The use of Independent Trader (IT) professionals by larger firms is a popular area of contracting out work. Rather than entrust tasks to medium-size or large specialist organisations, they turn to the self-employed individual expert, knowing full well that such a person will be only too grateful for the work and not be demanding payment of invoices every month. In some cases, it is not uncommon for a sole trader to be owed thousands of pounds for months at a time. Collecting these debts can be a frustrating task. It is not unusual, for instance, for larger firms to avoid payment to their contractors by disagreeing with the completed job. This leads to a protracted argument often with the client insisting that the job has not been completed as ordered. The end result is sometimes a refusal to pay.

The IT industry can be harder than most areas of business, as disputes are frequent. It is rarely easy to quantify what work has to be done, or what level of responsibility is expected of the contractor. The client may see the job in one way and the contractor in another. For example, self-employed trader Michael Mounteney experienced such a situation when a contract turned into a dispute after he left the source code of a system he developed for the in-house programmers to finish. He assumed that his part of the project was over and that the in-house programmers would take over. Unfortunately this was not the case, and the client insisted that Mr Mounteney had not completed the project and refused to pay up.

Kevin Jay, account controller of debt collectors European Collections and Investigations, describes independent trader debts as among the hardest to collect, with large firms looking for the slightest excuse to use as a reason for not paying. The answer for many IT contractors is to operate through an employment agency. By signing up with such an organisation the sole trader is in a stronger position, in that agencies are obliged by law to pay up as soon as they have received payment from the client. Furthermore, any disputes that arise are usually settled between the client and the agent. However, despite being in a stronger position working through an agency, hiccups can and do occur.

According to Doug Woodward, director of operations for Computer People, some agencies are worse than the clients, and actually illegally use contractors' money to assist their own cash-flow. Excuses given for late or non-payment vary from: 'The cheque is in the post.' to: 'The cheque was sent last week, and must be lost.' This state of affairs is not too common, but does occur from time to time. It is therefore sensible for all self-employed contractors considering employment via an agency to ensure they are confident that the firm is respectable and will not take them for a ride.

To avoid such problems, most contractors use informal networks of friends and specialist bulletin boards to check out new agencies. Doug Woodward suggests that contractors ask the agency for details of its customer base, turnover and profit. Also, check how long they have been in business. As a public company, Computer People is an IT employment agency with company accounts and other information readily available for inspection. As for paying contractors, they are paid weekly through BACS (Bankers' Automated Clearing Services).

Roger Sinclair, an IT lawyer, advocates making payment terms absolutely clear in all contracts. He suggests that it is best to give as little time as possible in any terms of payment. To grant 30 days could well lead to two, or even three months wait for settlement, so to avoid such a facility is a wise move on the behalf of the sole trader.

In practice, despite the intention of the trader to enter into only mutually arranged contracts, there will almost certainly be occasions when work is commenced on the verbal agreement of a trusted client. This happened to Michael Mounteney, who agreed to start a job on the strength of a verbal agreement with one of his clients. When it came to time for payment Mr Mounteney found that his trusted client refused to pay the previously verbally-agreed daily rate. A long-winded disagreement ensued that was eventually settled in the County Court, when the client was ordered to pay up in full.

The County Court was also helpful to a Mr Michael Atkinson, a contractor specialising in the oil, electricity and gas industries. Mr Atkinson ran into a dispute with his clients, the National Grid Company who withheld a considerable amount of money. After working on site for five months, Mr Atkinson had been paid for only four months work. There was no apparent reason to withhold fees, so Mr Atkinson resorted to a County Court Summons. His clients were ordered to pay up in full, plus all legal costs incurred in the issuing of the summons.

There are alternative methods of recovery besides a County Court Summons. One option is to issue what is known as a **Statutory Demand**. This course of action is the first step towards winding-up proceedings and is not something any solvent organisation will wish to get involved in. The slightest whisper of a reputable firm being wound-up could transmit shock waves through the business community that could ultimately affect new business in the offing. In one case, rumour of a Statutory Demand being served on a construction firm resulted in a loss to the company of a multi-million pound contract.

Under demand, the defendant is expected to pay the debt described within 21 days, and in the event that they do not do so then winding-up action is commenced. Of course, it goes without saying that if the defendant firm does not in fact have sufficient funds to settle the debt, then all creditors are going to have to wait their turn. Even then there will be no guarantee the debt will ever be settled.

A further option is to use the services of a **debt collection agency**. Firms like European Collections and Investigations, work on a no-collect-no-fee basis. *ECI* negotiates to take a percentage of any debt recovered, taking into account whether there is any dispute between the parties and how old the debt is. Private debt collection fees vary and are always dependant on the amount collected and the time taken to recover money. In some cases it has taken as long as two years to recover outstanding fees, in which case the agency fee could well be near the 45 per cent mark.

One safety measure a sole trader can try to take when conducting business transactions with corporate organisations is to obtain signed **personal undertakings** from directors who are willing to honour any debt outstanding at a time the company is unable to pay up. This means such guarantees can be exercised by creditors should a client go into liquidation. When seeking the personal indemnification of company directors it is also necessary to check out the creditworthiness of the said directors at the time of vetting the firm's financial stability.

All in all, the life of an independent trader is precarious, with some creditors attempting all manner of tricks to avoid their liabilities. To make matters worse, the Bankruptcy Courts are full of large and medium firms who have gone into liquidation. When this happens the chances of recovery for the sole operator are not very good. Hence the general advice given in points 1 to 7 above is doubly important for the self-employed.

2   Tracing Missing Debtors

The 'art' of tracing a missing person or company might also be described as in 'inexact science'. There are no official methods, just a few basic ground rules to refer to, and the 'hunter' has to rely on common sense and the numerous sources of information that can be used to trace the delinquent debtor. The first strategy, which is relatively cheap and easy to try before more arduous investigations, depends on whether the debtor has left a forwarding address with the post office.

Tracing an Address via the Postal Authorities

It is in fact not possible to obtain new addresses directly from Royal Mail: they are legally bound to secrecy. However, all is not lost because the following *legal* system can be adopted to obtain details of a forwarding address held by the postal authorities. The method now described applies to individuals and firms:

(a) Write to the last-known address, preferably using registered mail.
(b) When dispatching at the post office, request an **advice delivery** form.
(c) In cases where a re-direction address is held by the post office department, the appropriate sorting office will post on the registered envelope, along with the advice form on which the new address has been written.
(d) In due course the sender will receive the advice form

acknowledging that the registered letter has been delivered, and there will be the forwarding address readily available for the sender to utilise as necessary.

The above is the most expedient method of tracking down a missing person or firm. However, most cases are not so easy. Many people do not re-direct their mail, especially those who have good reason to avoid detection. It is on these occasions that more complicated methods of tracing are necessary. The basic choice to be made is between undertaking an independent, in-house search and employing the services of an external tracing agency or private investigator.

'Do-it-Yourself' Searching Strategy

The following advice applies primarily to a search for an individual or partnership – other tactics for tracing a limited company will be covered later.

1. **Electoral roll**   This valuable register is also referred to as the **voters list**. It is published every year by local councils and available for private examination at public libraries. In the event the debtor's address is not local to the creditor, then a *telephone call* to the library holding the electoral roll might reveal the information required. It should be appreciated that not all libraries are necessarily co-operative, it could well be that a request for information from the roll is declined.

Should this be the case, then one can also access the voters list by subscribing to any one of the credit reference agencies listed in the reference section. The creditor can check either by telephone, letter, or on-line the database of the credit reference agency, which will hold millions of names and addresses covering the UK. We shall discuss asking credit reference organisations to operate a **tracing service** in the next section of this chapter.

When checking the electoral register, the researcher should note all the names listed at the last known address. Sometimes the debtor's names are listed along with other names and possibly apartment numbers. All names should be recorded along with those of **neighbours**.

2. **Telephone directory enquiries**   Having compiled a list of names from the debtor's last known address, along with the names of neighbours, it is then a simple matter of cross-referring to telephone directory enquiries and confirming if any of the names are listed as telephone subscribers. British Telecom, the various cellular telephone companies and other communications firms operate a directory service so this task should be relatively straightforward. Unless, of course, the debtor is ex-directory in which case numbers will not be obtainable.

3. **Telephone research**   Having obtained telephone numbers for the debtor's last-known address, along with numbers for neighbours, the next step is to carry out telephone research to establish the forwarding address of the missing debtor. The initial tendency is for the inexperienced researcher to telephone the last-known address *first* and ask to speak to the debtor. This is definitely not the most productive method to adopt. It should be appreciated that debtors have a habit of misleading creditors in many ways. It is not difficult for someone to lie about their or others' identity or whereabouts.

The best tactic for finding the residents of a particular address is rather to contact **neighbours** first and to collate as much information as possible about the subject of enquiry. By speaking to neighbours it is possible to construct a detailed profile of the debtor *before* contacting the last known address, which might be just as well because he/she/they might still be resident at the address in question.

British Telecom Phone Base   A relatively new service, Phone Base enables telephone subscribers to access directly the British Telecom telephone directories database via the telephone line. With this service a subscriber can find names and addresses, as well as the phone numbers, for any listed phone-user in the UK. All this is available without calling a BT operator and all the subscriber requires is a suitable computer and modem for connecting to the service.

Phone Base is a dial-up service whereby the computer is connected to the database by way of a modem and the ordinary telephone network. All you require is: a personal computer

(PC); a modem connected to your telephone line (V23 compatible); communications software loaded on to your PC, i.e. Xtalk™ or Breakout™.

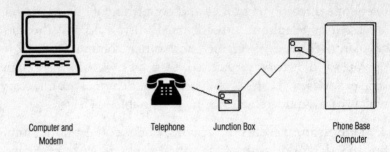

Computer and   Telephone   Junction Box   Phone Base
Modem   Computer

The database information is divided into two sections. The Business and Government section incorporates all manner of businesses, shops, industrial factories, local and national government departments and facilities. The Residential section contains home telephone numbers.

4. **Speaking with neighbours**   The job of extracting general information from someone about a neighbour is not an easy task. Discretion, politeness and a certain amount of mild deception are attributes the enquirer should possess. Before attempting any sort of deception, consult the section of this chapter concerning **cover stories**. The following information should be pursued:

(a)   Details of any close friends or relatives living in the area.

(b)   If no forwarding address has been left, then a clue as to the *area* will be useful.

(c)   Did the debtor *own* the last known address. If so, has it been sold by local agents and what solicitors did the conveyancing?

(d)   If the property was not owned, then who might the landlord, agents, or owners be?

(e)   Have there been any other callers seeking to contact the debtor? If so, obtain details, phone numbers, if available.

(f)   Where did the subject of enquiry work? If self-employed, trade name and any office address, also partner's details.

(g)   Have British Telecom, gas, electricity and/or water board been seeking to contact debtor?

(h)   If house is a council property, obtain the full address and phone number of local authority officer responsible for rent.

(i)   In the event the debtor has moved, are the residents currently living at the address related in any way?

(j)   It might transpire that the debtor had got himself into trouble with the police. If so, it could be that he is serving a prison sentence. Any clue as to when convicted and sentenced will assist in tracing the prison in which the subject is housed.

Obviously, to extract so much information from anyone is not likely to happen by just telephoning a couple of neighbours in a casual manner. Skilled questioning is required to obtain personal data of this kind. This is a very good reason to entrust the task of tracking missing persons and other investigations to a member of staff or independent agent who has experience of such work. However, if you are determined to do it yourself, it is likely that you will need a **cover story** (see section later in this chapter).

5. **Last known address** Having exhausted neighbouring sources, the time arrives to contact the debtor's last known address. However, if you know that the debtor is still resident at the address, then the job of tracing is successfully concluded. A telephone call to the address should not be necesssary. The next problem is how to collect the outstanding money owed, and this is covered in subsequent chapters.

If, on the other hand, enquiries have proved inconclusive or shown that the debtor no longer lives at the last known address it is necessary to telephone. If the debtor *might* still live there, *be careful*: *discreetly* question the answerer, have a cover story prepared and do not reveal the true reason for your call, or your identity, if the debtor or a house-sharer answers. You will have then established the debtor's whereabouts and can proceed with a collection strategy.

Should it transpire that the current occupants are in no way connected with the debtor, then a straightforward, polite request for a forwarding address may more than likely suffice. It is advisable to have available a questionnaire listing useful items of information that will assist in tracing the absconder.

Potential situations when contacting last known address:

(a) Absconder vanished, occupants not related but unable to assist.

(b) Occupants not connected but have a forwarding address and are willing to supply.

(c) Occupants related to debtor and are in possession of an address but unwilling to provide the same, however will pass messages.

(d) Occupants may well be the landlords of the property who are also seeking to trace the debtor. In such circumstances collaboration is worth considering.

Whatever situation is presented by the occupants of the last known address, attempts should be made (as already described) to collect as much information as possible relating to the circumstances of the debtor. Should it materialise that the address has been the subject of a building society eviction and repossession, identities of local agents, lawyers and the society will be useful in tracking down the absconder.

6. **Further research required?** If, after telephoning neighbours and the last known address, concrete information has not been forthcoming, now is the time to collate and review whatever data has been obtained for analysis and further enquiries. Depending on what information on a customer is held by the creditor, there might be other sources of investigation, such as previous addresses, past employers, and referees, listed on an agreement signed by the customer. Obviously, the creditor who had taken the trouble during the initial stage of the business relationship to check out the customer stands a better chance of tracking them down.

Here is a review of possible sources, with an evaluation of their potential fruitfulness – summarised by a 'potential success rating' (PSR), from 1 to 10.

(a) *Close friends and relatives*   Such sources are sometimes very co-operative. The not so co-operative can be 'persuaded' (legally) to impart information. *PSR:*   **8**

(b) *Area of residency known but no address*   Such clues can be of use, especially if the subject of enquiry has an unusual surname and is a telephone subscriber. By carrying out an on-line computer search via British Telecom's directory enquiry service, a search of a specific area could well reveal a new address. *PSR:*   **6**

(c) *Estate agents and solicitors*   Such organisations are secretive and generally not co-operative. Estate agents will normally reveal their client's solicitors and that is all. Solicitors will probably pass on a letter to the debtor and it might even be possible to arrange a meeting. *PSR:*   **4**

(d) *Landlords*   Useful sources and normally helpful, especially when owed money by the absconder. Such sources could also know of relatives, or employers might also have taken out references. *PSR:*   **8**

(e) *Other creditors*   Invaluable sources of assistance, especially when they are made aware that collaboration might be mutually beneficial. *PSR:*   **8**

(f) *Former employers*   Another good source of information. Depending on the absconder's job, some kind of legally harmless cover story may be required. *PSR:*   **7**

(g) *Privatised utilities' accounts departments* (i.e. BT, gas, water, electricity)   It is difficult to obtain assistance from these organisations. All data is kept on computer and subject to the Data Protection Act. *PSR:*   **3**

(h) *Local councils*   Sometimes quite helpful. Some information from such sources is legally available to the public, alternatively some councils will provide 'off the record' assistance. *PSR:*   **7**

(i) *Police and Prison Service*   Best approached via solicitors. Official Secrets Act inhibits the assisting of private persons. *PSR:*   **2**

(j) *Banks and building societies*   Not good sources. *PSR:*   **1**

Cover Stories

A cover story is best described as a distortion of the truth, or a complete prefabrication, with the purpose of obtaining information which, on occasions, can be presented in evidence in a court of law. It could well turn out that the evidence obtained is not admissible and the activator of the cover story has in fact committed a criminal offence. It therefore goes without saying that when it is decided to adopt a cover story, great care should be taken when deceiving anyone for the purpose of collecting information such as forwarding addresses of debtors. A good cover story is legal, ethical and simple but imaginative.

Illegal cover stories   To pose as any official person, i.e. police officer, DSS officer, or an Inland Revenue official, could result in prosecution. Under no circumstances should a private person pose in any manner that could be considered illegal. There are numerous legal methods of operation that, with a little imagination, can result in success.

Unethical cover stories   Some private investigators and debt-collectors, whilst not breaking the law, do have a tendency to be unethical or immoral in their presentation of cover stories. It is not uncommon for such individuals to lead sources into believing that the subject of investigation stands to inherit millions from a death in the family. Taking the deception a stage further, it is also a 'trick' of such deceivers' craft to lead neighbours, friends and employers into believing that the debtor's next of kin has had a serious accident and the former's attendance is required at a hospital. While such methods can be, and are, regularly successful, they are despicable and should never be contemplated during the tracing or investigating of a debtor.

Acceptable cover stories   There are numerous harmless cover stories that, if carefully conducted, will result in the successful acquisition of information. Here are a few examples:

(a)   Looking for one's lost relative who is thought to be a friend of the debtor.

(b) Debtor witnessed (not involved in) a *minor* traffic accident and it is essential to speak with him in order to settle an insurance claim.

(c) Personal delivery of flowers to a female debtor.

(d) Personal delivery of another gift to a male or female debtor.

(e) Debtor has won free tickets in the national lottery from a private firm; to actually purchase such tickets would support the cover story.

The above examples are just a few of the legal cover stories currently in use by private investigators. With a little thought, anyone should be able to conceive a suitable, harmless pretext.

Finally, it is worth noting that phone research might not be possible. Then, the only other method is to physically attend the last known address. On such occasions investigative tactics are to note details of all motor vehicles that appear to be associated with the last known address; to intercept the local postman; and to visit the local dairy and newsagents can also result in clues being obtained.

Such endeavours can be difficult, time-consuming, unnerving and even dangerous (as can phone research). Hence, one must always consider the option of employing or enlisting the services of an experienced specialist. An in-house 'tracer' can be worth much more than an annual salary to an organisation with a continuing requirement to trace missing customers. This, of course, is probably feasible only for larger companies. The alternative is to contract out such work to a tracing firm or detective agency (see later section).

Tracing a Limited Company

From the outset it has to be said that, even though it is possible to trace a limited company this does not guarantee the successful recovery of a debt. In the event directors have signed personal guarantees on the debt, then the chances of recovery are of course better.

The first and most valuable source of company information is

Companies House where all information relating to the formation and operation of British registered companies is held. Access to this data is available direct, or via any one of the search organisations in the United Kingdom. This information includes:

- Address of registered office
- Annual audited accounts
- Details of accountants
- Names and addresses of directors and shareholders and secretary, plus other directorships
- Mortgages and other charges, plus bankers
- Objects of the company
- Liquidators and/or receivers appointed

In the event a limited company vanishes, then tracing such a firm should not prove too difficult. By acquiring the company file and analysing the considerable amount of available information, the possibility of a successful trace is very good.

The first port of call should be a telephone call to the accountants, who will be able to confirm if their clients are still trading and where. Should the company have been wound-up for any reason, then the appropriate notification will be displayed on the file, including the details of the liquidator or receiver, from where assistance is usually forthcoming. Should the accountants not be co-operative for any particular reason, then enquiries directed to the private addresses of the directors, shareholders or secretary will be required, using the method described in the previous section.

The most productive story that can be used in tracing a limited company is for the creditor to lead everyone to believe that they are a potential client of the missing firm who is seeking to do business with them. If the firm is still trading, then it will be quite easy to encourage a source to reveal the current trading address.

Potential Situations

(a) *Company has moved address but still trading* There should be no difficulty in tracing via British Telecom, or the accountants listed on the company file.

(b) *Company ceased trading but not officially wound-up*   Accountants should be able to clarify the situation, as should the directors, secretary and shareholders.

(c) *Company has been wound-up*   Most receivers or liquidators will assist creditors with a claim.

(d) *Company has adopted another title*   This is a popular trick adopted by unscrupulous directors to avoid creditors. Without the signed personal guarantee of directors, recovery is normally difficult. However, if it can be proved that the new company is linked to the original operation, then it should be possible to 'encourage' directors to honour obligations. Such situations are covered in detail in the next chapter.

Tracking down a delinquent limited company is usually quite straightforward, unless the directors have been involved in systematic fraud via the use of false names and addresses, in which case a creditor is in for a hard time. Chapter four covers the various courses open to the victim of such a situation. Such unfortunate circumstances highlight the benefits of carrying out in-depth initial enquiries into the background and operations of any potential limited company client *before* granting credit facilities.

Should it transpire that the directors named on the delinquent company file are also listed as directors of other limited companies, then this will provide more sources of information to approach in the hunt for the missing firm. It is not uncommon for individuals to hold several directorships. In the event such information is available then approaches to the other companies listed might reveal useful clues as to the current status of missing organisations. It will be necessary to obtain copies of the additional companies files in order to contact particular directors. The most comprehensive sources of any sort of company information are the various branches of Companies House (see page 160).

Balance Sheets

ABC's balance sheet below indicates that the funds available at the beginning of the year totalled £1,748,546 and came from:–

	£
Share Capital	240,000
Retained profits and reserves	1,038,746
Long-term loan	280,000
Deferred Taxation	189,800
	1,748,546

Viewed from the other side of the balance sheet, these funds were represented by:

		£
Fixed Assets		908,768
Investments		44,000
Current Assets	1,701,192	
Less: current liabilities	905,414	
		795,778
		1,748,546

Profit and Loss Account of a Financial Sound Company

ABC LIMITED
Comprehensive Profit and Loss Account for the
year ended December 1991

	£	1990 %	£	1991 %
Sales	4,849,800	100	3,986,800	100
Costs of Sales:				
Materials	2,670,434	55.1	2,210,380	55.4
Wages	902,514	18.6	661.332	16.6
	3,572,948	73.7	2,871,712	72.0
Gross profit	1,276,852	26.3	1,115,088	28.0
Overhead expenses:				
Production	581,638	11.9	465,286	11.7
Distribution	197,274	4.1	144,010	3.6
Administrative	213,074	4.4	212,156	5.3
	991,986	20.4	821,452	20.6
Net operating profit, before interest & taxation	284,866	5.9	293,636	7.4

XYZ LIMITED
Balance Sheet
31 December 1992

FIXED ASSETS		
Tangible assets	488,061	454,384
Investments	26,000	22,000
	541,061	476,384
CURRENT ASSETS		
Stocks	435,289	404,095
Debtors	584,537	416,756
Cash	26,333	29,745
	1,046,159	850,596
CREDITORS: AMOUNTS FALLING DUE WITHIN ONE YEAR		
Bank Overdraft	111,966	85,599
Trade creditors	461,958	329,877
Taxation	46,061	16,831
Dividend	21,600	20,400
	641,585	452,707
NET CURRENT ASSETS	404,574	397,889
TOTAL ASSETS LESS CURRENT LIABILITIES	918,635	874,273
CREDITORS: AMOUNTS FALLING DUE AFTER MORE THAN ONE YEAR		
Long term loan	(140,000)	(140,000)
PROVISIONS FOR LIABILITIES AND CHARGES		
Deferred taxation	(99,107)	(94,900)
	679,528	639,373
CAPITAL AND RESERVES		
Called-up share capital	120,000	120,000
Share premium account	243,336	243,336
Profit and loss account	316,192	276,037
	679,528	639,373

Private Investigation Agencies

The use of such organisations to check out customers, and debtors, is now an accepted part of business operations. Most areas of industry, commerce and the legal profession regularly engage the services of 'private eyes'. Even government departments employ private detectives and security firms on long-term assignments; private policing is an integral part of modern government and business activity.

This use of such individuals and organisations from a fraternity that is only partially regulated is a very contentious subject. So much so that there have been numerous attempts from within the profession to persuade the government to introduce legislation to control Britain's private police. So far all have failed, although at the time of writing parliamentary discussions are again taking place.

To the first-time user, the task of deciding on a private investigation agency is very difficult. There is no central register or official organisation to consult. Similarly, by the very nature of the work, to obtain references from satisfied trade clients is almost impossible; although on occasions solicitors can be approached to testify as to the ethics and ability of investigators used within the legal profession. It has to be said that the wrong choice can and almost certainly will cause inconvenience and financial loss. It could amount to throwing good money after bad.

Conversely, the correct choice can be beneficial in many ways. Speedy tracing of missing debtors, professional handling of confidential investigations and expert advice that, coming from legal sources could well cost thousands of pounds.

In such cases, employing an ethical, skilled firm of private investigators is a lot more economical than instructing a solicitor. For example, tracking down missing hire purchase customers: in exchange for a regular supply of work, most investigation agencies will operate a fixed fee for tracing investigations. Some even operate a *no-trace-no-fee* policy. Eurotec, for example, cover the whole of the United Kingdom and charge around £80 for a tracing enquiry and/or general investigations relating to debts and other consumer problems. As the reason for a particular investigation changes and the type of assignment changes, this results in fees increasing accordingly, depending on the circumstances surrounding a particular investigation. Protracted investigations of a specialist nature normally cost the client an hourly rate plus mileage and other expenses; £30 per hour plus thirty pence a mile would not be considered unreasonable.

Choosing a Private Investigator

The absence of effective official regulation of the detective industry has resulted in a proliferation of 'cowboys' setting up agencies that in some cases have been fronts for other criminal activity. Clients are regularly fleeced by these unscrupulous types, who are usually totally unqualified. The potential client must take precautions.

The first sensible step is to contact **The Association of British Investigators** (ABI), whose address can be found on pages 160 and 163. With origins dating back to 1913, the ABI is now recognised as the premier professional body for private investigators working in the United Kingdom. Two dates are particularly significant in the history of the ABI. In 1953, the British Detective Association amalgamated with the Federation of British Detectives to form the Association of British Detectives. In 1970, the Association became a corporate body and assumed its current title.

Throughout its long history, the ABI has workd hard to improve the standing and reputation of the investigative profession, sponsoring a number of landmark initiatives, including the lobbying of Parliament and the Home Office for a form of statutory control. It is no accident that the ABI is now regarded as the mouthpiece of the profession, insisting as it does on carefully selecting each and every member. All applicants are stringently examined and scrutinised as to their knowledge, competence and ethics. They are also required to adhere to a strict code of ethics, monitored by a Disciplinary Committee.

There are ABI members located in most parts of the UK, and in many overseas countries as well. Often, ABI investigators will collaborate on a particular case. They will provide local knowledge or information, frequently saving a client both time and money. This pooling of resources is a key feature of the work of the Association. So too are the many seminars and workshops that the ABI organises on a regular basis. These are designed to maintain standards and to provide a regular flow of information to the regional membership. A wide range of topics are covered, including changes to the law, and the latest trends and developments in techniques and equipment.

The result is a team of modern professionals who are properly trained, completely reliable and totally committed to providing the client with a first-class service.

Code of ethics   Every ABI investigator must abide by the following code of ethics:

1. To perform all professional duties in accordance with the highest moral principles and never be guilty of conduct which will bring reproach upon the profession of the private investigator or the Association of British Investigators.
2. To verify the credentials of clients and that they have lawful and moral reasons to instruct an investigation.
3. To respect the privacy of clients and their lawful confidences.
4. To ensure that the services are adequately secure to protect privacy and to guard against inadvertent disclosure of private information.
5. To ensure that all employees and persons paid to assist in investigation adhere to this code of ethics and accept responsibility thereof.
6. To conduct all investigations within the bounds of legality, morality and professional ethics.
7. To respect the best interests of clients by maintaining the highest standard of proficiency and reporting to our clients all the facts ascertained whether they are advantageous or detrimental, with nothing being withheld from the clients save by the dictates of law.
8. To work together with all members of the Association towards the achievement of the highest professional objectives of the Association and to observe the principles of truth, accuracy and prudence.

Services These are just some of the many services an ABI investigator can provide:

- Personnel screening
- Investigation of internal thefts
- Insurance fraud surveillance
- Accident investigation
- Checking company credentials
- Uncovering patent violations
- Countering industrial espionage
- Fraudulent claim investigation
- Process serving
- Tracing missing persons

3   Dealing with Debtors

To sue or not to sue, that is the question. In most cases the first reaction of the creditor is to place the collection of a debt into the hands of solicitors who are relied upon to collect outstanding monies. What some creditors fail to realise is that by utilising solicitors more costs will be incurred and that there is no guarantee that the legal process will result in the debtor paying up. It is a fact of business life that there are hundreds of cases a year concluded in court where considerable costs have been incurred by the creditor who has used solicitors, and the debtor has failed and/or refused to honour his obligation.

What usually happens in such cases is that the lawyer advises the client to bankrupt the debtor. Alternatively the creditor is advised that it is a waste of time pursuing the debt. The result of such situations is that the client is considerably out of pocket and the solicitor . . . has earned a healthy fee chasing after money he should have realised was not available. Creditors should be aware that even in the event a Court Order is obtained, this does not guarantee payment by the debtor.

Pre-sue Advice

Before resorting to any form of costly litigation there are a number of courses of action that can and should be considered by creditors:

(1) Having located the missing individual or firm, a clearly presented letter demanding payment of the debt should be sent to the debtor. It is advisable to enclose a copy of the account.

(2) In the event the debtor fails to respond then it would not be unreasonable to pay the cost of a **Solicitor's letter**, in the hope that this will encourage some movement towards settlement.

(3) If, after the above demands, the debtor still fails to honour his/her obligation, then there are three courses of action that can be considered:

(a) Resort to costly litigation via the use of a solicitor.
(b) Activate litigation **in person**, thus avoiding legal costs.
(c) Utilise the services of **private debt collectors** who operate on a commission basis.

Debtors' Ability to Pay

Before *any* move is made to collect a debt it is important that the creditor makes enquiries into the debtor's current financial status, the object of the exercise being to confirm the delinquent customer's ability, or inability, to settle the amount outstanding. After all, attempts to collect debts will be a complete waste of time should it transpire the debtor is completely broke and about to have their home and car repossessed. Conversely, if it is found that the debtor is enjoying a high standing of living, the case deserves persistence.

Looking into a debtor's lifestyle is simple and if conducted correctly will result in a clear picture of his current circumstances. It does however require the enquirer to be accurate otherwise the whole exercise could well be a waste of time. Collecting the following information will be useful.

Residence   The first move is to visit the individual's address for the purpose of confirming whether the private residence is owned or rented by the debtor. This should be a reasonably easy task;

discreet questions with neighbours should reveal ownership details. To ensure beyond any shadow of doubt that what has been uncovered is accurate, a public search of the appropriate **Land Registry** will confirm the names of all parties holding an interest in the debtor's address.

Depending on the exact type of relationship between the creditor and debtor, it is possible that a considerable amount of information was obtained before granting the facilities which led to the debt. For example, if the creditor is a bank or similar organisation then details of the private address should be held.

Assets and income   In order for a creditor to successfully collect a debt, details of assets and income are essential to the claim. A private residence is normally the most valuable asset and most debtors, when faced with the threat of a **Legal Charge** on their home, will pay up or at least contact the claimant with a suggestion to settle. It is therefore important that accurate and probing enquiries are carried out into the ownership of the debtor's private abode.

Other useful assets that can be legally seized by Officers of the Court (if and when a Court Order is granted) include motor vehicles, furniture, antiques and domestic and private items. The most convenient asset to consider seizing with the assistance and authority of the court is a motor vehicle. However, it should be remembered many such items are normally purchased on some kind of credit agreement, so there is always a strong possibility that a vehicle being used by the defendant is the legal property of a hire purchase company.

Motor vehicle enquiries are straightforward and should be conducted in the following manner:

1. First it is crucial to obtain the **registration number** of the defendant's private car. This can be done by visiting his private address late at night or very early in the morning or weekends, these being occasions when an individual's vehicle can normally be observed and the registration number noted. In the event the car is out of sight or parked in a garage, then an early morning visit will have to be made and a watch kept on the address until the debtor uses the car.

2. Once details of the car have been obtained an application will
    have to be made to the **DVLC, Swansea**, for written
    confirmation of the registered user. It should be remembered
    that the **registered user** is not always the **legal owner**. It
    will therefore be necessary to carry out further enquiries into
    the status of the vehicle. This can be done by enlisting the
    services of a private investigator who has access to hire
    purchase information (HPI).

3. Should the services of an external agent not be desired at this
    stage then a direct application can be made for HPI by the
    creditor who should contact the address listed on page 163.
    The information available from this source will clearly identify
    the circumstances of the vehicle and any financial and/or
    legal interest held by a hire purchase or similar organisation.
    The debtor should then be able to proceed accordingly if and
    when a court judgement is obtained.

Employment   In all cases of debt recovery, if a debtor is
unemployed then a creditor will be inhibited from settling a
claim. It is therefore essential to confirm details of employment
before activating any course of legal action. There are a few
methods of tracking a debtor to his place of work but some are
considered unethical. General examples are:

(1) Visit the address and discreetly question neighbours. It is
     sometimes possible to identify a place of work by such
     enquiries. However, beware: the debtor could get to hear
     that these enquiries have been made and this could result in
     all manner of inconvenient situations developing.

(2) Visit or telephone the debtor's address when he is certainly
     absent to 'extract' information out of a spouse or other
     member of the family. To do this will almost certainly
     require a **cover story**.

Other liabilities   In addition to targeting the assets and employers of a debtor, it would also be prudent to carry out County
Court judgement searches to confirm the existence of any other
outstanding liabilities. Such a search could also indicate if the

individual is in the habit of frequently incurring debts. This type of 'intelligence' will be invaluable when deciding on future courses of action.

Collecting Debts from Limited Companies

Procedures for collecting outstanding debts from limited companies differ in that there are some special considerations which affect the creditor's modus operandi. Limited companies are registered with the appropriate authority in accordance with current legislation. This means that the directors of such companies are obliged by law to comply with numerous regulations laid down by the **Companies Act**. These circumstances can be used to the advantage of the creditor. With a basic knowledge of company law and procedures, directors of debtor firms can be encouraged to realise that it is in *their personal interests* to arrange settlement of a company debt.

The business of checking on company assets in relation to motor vehicles and ownership of property is similar to that for an individual. All the creditor has to do is visit business addresses and carry out discreet enquiries with regard to the actual ownership of a business address. Normally managing agents, if not on the premises, are easy to locate. A careful approach to such organisations will normally reveal who the owners of a business address are.

Another valuable source of information is the **company file** of the debtor firm, on which might be recorded details of property owned that has been used as security for overdrafts, mortgages or other loans. As with domestic property, it is more than likely a bank or other finance house will hold legal charges on any address displayed on the company file. However it could well be that there is sufficient equity to be used for the settlement of the debt.

Also contained on the company file should be up to date **audited accounts** which show sufficient information to enable interested parties to appreciate exactly the state of the company financially, especially with regard to pre-tax profits. In the event the company has been put into **liquidation**, then an official notice will be included on the file. This should record the liquidator, who can then be approached and the debt lodged for inclusion in the settlement of the firm's affairs by the receiver if, or when, one has been appointed.

In cases where the debtor firm is still trading, then a visit to the business address will enable the creditor to note any other **plant or machinery** associated with the firm. Skilled investigators can talk their way into offices to observe other assets such as computers and business equipment. It is important to understand that debtors' goods cannot generally be seized without the authority of a court. Details of this process are included in subsequent sections of this book.

Breach of the Companies Act   If during pre-sue enquiries it transpires that audited accounts and annual returns are not up to date, then it is more than likely that directors of the debtor firm have committed criminal offences, for which they could be prosecuted. There might even be lodged on the file a warning from the authorities demanding that certain courses of action be activated within a certain time. If such a situation exists then this could be a warning that the firm is about to cease trading and that liquidation is on the cards. This is not a healthy situation for creditors to find themselves in, and invariably (depending on the amount of money involved) calls for extreme and expedient courses of action. The long-winded procedures of formal litigation are not really appropriate for such circumstances.

Debt Collectors

One course of action that could be appropriate is the use of private business debt collectors. Many such firms operate on a 'no-collect-no-fee' basis. Unfortunately this kind of business operation encourages all manner of unethical and highly illegal acts during the course of chasing a debt. Having said that, there *are* agencies around who are effective and reputable.

One rather imaginative firm used an operative dressed as a filthy tramp to collect outstanding invoices from a multi-million pound organisation with a reputation for keeping the smaller traders waiting for their money. The method was simple and one hundred per cent effective. The 'tramp', who was in fact a student, would dress in the dirtiest clothes one could imagine. Complete with false beard, and smelling of urine and excreta, he would present himself to the receptionist of the debtor company, present her with a copy of the invoice and a letter from the creditor demanding payment. He would then sit down and wait and if necessary, wait and wait . . . and wait. Polite and legal, the 'collector' would simply ensure that all concerned were aware he had no intention of moving *until he received payment*. On occasions, when threatened with the police, he would simply agree that perhaps they should be called, he would then produce a cellular telephone and dial the local newspaper.

Whilst this method might be considered unusual and extreme, it was not illegal, and whether or not it was unethical is arguable. Whatever it was, it was certainly effective.

Illegal Methods   As well as being unorthodox, the following examples of debt collection are highly illegal and not methods adopted by reputable firms.

1.   In 1991, a London businessman vanished owing over a quarter of a million pounds to a creditor. The debtor had been a director in a large company that had gone into liquidation owing millions. Although not personally respon- sible for the debts, one creditor did not see it that way and hired the services of a private detective. Operating on a 'no- collect-no-fee' basis, the private eye tracked the debtor down to a luxury hotel in Israel, where he bugged the absconder's telephone. Within a few days it was discovered that the debtor held a Swiss bank account into which he had diverted funds from the liquidated company.

   In the early hours of the morning the detective gained access to the hotel bedroom, where he abducted the debtor at gun-point and took him to the roof of the building. Holding a gun to his head, the detective gave the debtor the impression that should he fail to agree to travel to the location of his secret bank account then he would be shot and pushed off the hotel roof. Five days later the creditor was the happy recipient of the full amount of the debt.

2. Another even more bizarre example of illegal debt collection was the case of a stockbroker who misused investments of a firm connected to organised crime. Having lost millions of pounds the debtor took to his heels, hoping to evade detection in America. What he did not know was that the creditors were well connected in the USA, so much so it eventually became known throughout American crime syndicates that the debt was due.

    In due course the debtor was kidnapped off the streets, taken to a safe-house where he was threatened and eventually tortured to the point of death. Within a few days he had produced every penny of the missing millions and handed it over to people he thought were representing the creditors. This was not in fact the case, and when confronted by the genuine creditors failed miserably to convince them the debt had been paid. To this day the debtor is still suffering from injuries inflicted on him by these ruthless businessmen, who incidentally are still taking a cut from all that is earned by the debtor, who has been able to start up another business. With the threat of death hanging over him he is now faced with a lifetime of paying back his creditors.

Within reason, it is up to the creditor what sort of method he adopts to recover a debt. Obviously his own code and ethics will play a part in deciding how to deal with such financial problems. Some businesses still resort to using the numerous illegal collectors operating in the United Kingdom: former French Foreign Legion soldiers and other Special Forces types are asked to break legs and even (for the right price) kill an absconding debtor who is unable or unwilling to honour a financial obligation. Such courses of action, or any sort of 'scare tactic', should never be contemplated.

For the ethical and more down-to-earth creditor the following *legal* course of action via the County Court is available.

How to Sue in a County Court

A creditor who wishes to utilise the auspices of a court of law to recover outstanding debts can engage a solicitor or **act in person**.

The following information will help a creditor to act on their own behalf when resorting to litigation.

First it should be appreciated that just because the creditor insists an amount of money is owed does not mean that the court will automatically agree the debt. It is up to the creditor to prove to the court that the debt was properly created and is in fact outstanding. This should not be too difficult for the claimant who has maintained detailed records and copies of all invoices.

A visit to the County Court with all of the relevant paperwork and a chat with the normally helpful staff is all that is required to start the legal ball rolling. Once it is agreed that the creditor does in fact have a genuine claim, then self-explanatory application forms will have to be completed. At first sight they might look nothing more than civil service gobbledegook, however with the assistance of court staff these forms are easily dealt with and the wheels set in motion.

Here is a stage-by-stage guide to a typical litigation.

Stage one It will be necessary to complete three copies of a **Default Summons** form N1, one each for:

- the claimant who will be known as the **Plaintiff** from this point on
- the court
- the court to send to the debtor who will be referred to as the **Defendant**

In the event the claim is against more than one person, then copies of the form N1 will be required for each of them. The County Court will supply all of the above forms free of charge, and although staff are not solicitors they are usually very helpful to plaintiffs acting in person. It should be remembered that **legal advice** is not available from court staff; however there are numerous brochures that clearly describe the procedures required to activate a claim in person.

Stage two On completion of form N1 the Plaintiff will be required to pay a fee which will be governed by the scale in use at that particular time. Such charges are nothing like those charged by solicitors, in any event by acting in person the Plaintiff will have avoided legal expenses which would have been required in addition to the court costs.

Once the fee is paid to the court the summons is issued and a **case number**, sometimes referred to as a **plaint number**, is allocated to the action. The Plaintiff is also issued with a receipt on a form N205A which is called a **Notice of Issue**.

Stage three   The next stage in the proceedings is that the court will post a copy of the summons and a reply form N9A and B to the Defendant, who has 14 days to return the reply form. The 14 days actually commence on the day after the Defendant receives the summons.

On receipt of the summons there are various courses of action open to the Defendant:

- He can ignore the summons and not bother to respond

- He can return a copy of the form N9A admitting the debt, along with an offer to pay either in full or by instalments

- He can return the form N9B admitting only part of the debt

- He can return the form N9B denying the debt; on such occasions it sometimes transpires that the Defendant presents a counter claim

NB   It is important in all litigation cases that Defendants are fully and accurately informed of impending claims against them. If a Defendant can (and they often do) convince the court that he was not aware of what was happening, then cases usually cannot proceed until duplicate papers are issued and brought to the notice of the Defendant.

The process of ensuring that the Defendant has received the summons is always referred to as *serving* the documents, and a posting is usually the initial and certainly the most economical method to start with.

If, for whatever reason, sending the summons is not possible or recommended, then **personal service** is a popular method of ensuring the Defendant has received the summons. This is done either by a bailiff of the court, in which case an additional fee will be required. A better method of ensuring service is completed on the Defendant is to entrust the task to a private 'process server' or investigation agency: in cases where Defendants are prone to dodging their creditors this is by far the most productive way of dealing with such debtors.

Once service has been successfully concluded, it is usual for the person responsible for the service to attend the court (or a solicitor) for the purpose of swearing on oath to the fact service has been concluded. This statement is prepared in an **affidavit**, which then becomes part and parcel of the Plaintiff's case file.

Stage four   When it has been established that service has been concluded, and following the 14-day period allowed to the Defendant, the Plaintiff is then able to progress the claim. However, this is not a speedy procedure owing to the fact there are hundreds of claims waiting to be heard at any one time. It should also be remembered that the wheels of justice have never been known to turn quickly. From this point, progress will be governed by the attitude of the Defendant. For example, in a lot of cases, once the summons has been served, it is not unusual for the Plaintiff to receive full settlement of the outstanding debt. The thought of being dragged through the courts can be too much for a Defendant who fully realises that they cannot avoid the debt.

Should it be that the Defendant does *not* pay the full amount and only admits part of the claim, then it is up to the Plaintiff to decide if it will be worthwhile to proceed; it could well be that rather than get involved in a protracted legal dispute, it might be worthwhile accepting what is on offer.

The worst scenario that can develop following service of the summons, is that the debt is either denied or ignored. This means the Plaintiff is in the position of having to resort to what could turn out to be a real trial of not only the case, but also one's patience. At least by acting in person, expensive solicitor's costs will not be involved.

Stage five   For the purpose of discussion, let us imagine the Defendant has acknowledged service of the summons but denies the whole of the debt. It will then be necessary for the Plaintiff to go to trial which, depending on the amount being claimed and the kind of case being dealt with, might involve an **arbitration**

hearing. In most cases the Arbitrator will be a District Judge, who will oversee the case in the presence of both the Plaintiff and the Defendant. It is therefore essential that the claimant has prepared all evidence in the form of documents for examination at the hearing. If there are any letters or statements from witnesses it is important to confirm that such documents are signed by anyone who is a possible witness.

The claimant should be quite clear as to what they wish to present at the hearing, and if necessary prepare a written outline of the facts for their own use. It is important to appreciate that this will be an occasion when the Plaintiff will be obliged to prove to the court that the debt is genuine. Failure to convince the Arbitrator will almost certainly result in the case being terminated. This of course means the debtor could well escape his obligation. Having said that, it is possible to appeal and there are other legal courses of action that, depending on the size of the debt, can be adopted.

Stage six   How does the Arbitrator decide? He or she will listen to, or read the evidence produced by the Plaintiff and Defendant. This will include details of the debt and any statements submitted by witnesses who may well have to be called and examined. In most cases the Arbitrator will hear the Plaintiff's claim first and then allow the Defendant to comment. Both parties will be allowed to comment and cross-examine each other. When the court has heard all the evidence, the Arbitrator will then announce the decision that has been reached. This is called the **Award**.

At this stage it will be useful for both parties to make notes as to the reasons for the award; this will help if at any time in the future it is decided by either party to appeal against the decision. This decision will be made on the basis of legal procedures and the evidence, which can be in three forms: **Spoken**, **Written** and **Expert** evidence.

It is important to note that in all cases where the evidence of a witness is involved, it will be necessary for the Arbitrator to question what the witness has to say. It will not be possible or advisable for the Plaintiff to answer questions on behalf of a witness, it is therefore sensible for any witness involved in a dispute to be present at the hearing. They can then be questioned direct and their evidence duly assessed as to its worth.

An alternative method of dealing with a Plaintiff's claim is for the court to decide to allow a trial by either a Circuit or District Judge. This would entail a hearing in a courtroom (called **Open Court**) which members of the public and press are allowed to attend. The case could also be heard in Judges' Chambers, in which case only those involved in the trial would be allowed to attend.

If the case is heard in Open Court then the judge will wear robes and a wig, in Chambers ordinary clothes would be required. Addressing the judge, one is expected to use the title 'your Honour' for a Circuit Judge and simply 'Sir' or 'Madam' for a District Judge. Apart from that, the procedures of presenting evidence are as at an arbitration hearing. See the final chapter of this book for further advice on courtroom tactics.

Stage seven   In the event the judge decides in favour of the Plaintiff, then the court will award what is referred to as a **Judgement** against the Defendant who can if he so wishes apply to have the finding set aside while he prepares an appeal. However the court will not accept such an application at the drop of a hat, good reasons have to be given before an appeal is allowed to proceed.

Shortly following the judge's decision, the court will complete a Judgement Order form N30 which informs the Defendant of the full nature of the debt now due, also when and how to go about paying. At this stage the Defendant is under the jurisdiction of the court and, depending on his handling of the situation, from this point could find himself in all manner of situations. The Creditor is now in a much stronger position than he was before the case was heard. Also, by acting *in person*, only a minimal amount of money has been spent. Had a solicitor been used to reach this stage, there is no telling what legal costs would have been amassed. It is not uncommon for costs in civil cases of this nature to run into thousands of pounds, especially on occasions when a lawyer suggests the use of barristers to benefit the case.

Stage eight   It is not unusual for stubborn or corrupt types to avoid judgements awarded against them. Deception and misrepresentation are all part and parcel of avoiding the issue. However, if the Plaintiff has prepared the case and claim correctly, and has the current address and circumstances of the debtor to hand, then progressing with the judgement is possible and should not be too difficult. It must be said however that some degree of inconvenience will be experienced.

Once a successful judgement is obtained, the first move is to ensure that the Defendant has been delivered of or had served on him the Judgement Form N30. On this document will be a date by which the debt must be paid to the Plaintiff. In the event this is not adhered to then certain courses of action will have to be activated to recover the outstanding debt plus costs which will by now have been awarded against the Defendant:

Attachment of earnings   The most effective and popular method of executing the judgement, is to apply to the court for an order to withhold regular amounts of money from the Defendant's salary – an **Attachment of Earnings**. Once again, the process is simple and involves another application to the court which, on occasions when Defendants have ignored judgements awarded against them, will normally issue an Attachment without too much procrastination.

The application for an Attachment, once completed by the Plaintiff, will show full details of the judgement debt, along with the Defendant's employers. Once the actual Order is issued, it then has to be served on the Defendant's company or the Defendant. Ideally, personal service should be effected; this will reduce the risk of suggestion that the document was not received by the employers.

Once the Attachment of Earnings is up and running then it should only be a short time before the payments are received by the creditor. It should be noted that such an Order cannot be made if the Defendant is:

- self employed or unemployed
- a firm or limited company
- a serving member of the Armed Forces
- a merchant seaman

Should the Defendant in fact be a serving member or the forces or the merchant navy, then special rules for executing judgement against their employers apply, details of which can be obtained from the court.

NB   In all cases where an Attachment of Earning is being taken out, the Plaintiff can request an **index search** which covers all existing County Court and Magistrate cases where Attachments are in force. Should it transpire that there is already such an Order in force against the Defendant, then the more recent judgement can be included on that Order.

Warrant of Execution   Another course of action that can cause great inconvenience to a debtor is to apply for a **Warrant of Execution** that authorises court bailiffs to seize personal items belonging to the debtor. Such goods are then sold at auction, and what money is realised is passed onto the creditor.

Normally a motor vehicle that holds suitable equity, after say the HP Company have been paid off, is taken by the bailiff. Should the Defendant not have a vehicle, then the bailiff is entitled to take away any other personal item from the private residence, but only if the debtor allows the court official entry to the property. Unfortunately a court bailiff generally does not have power to force his way into a person's home in such cases.

Interrogation of the debtor   This procedure is a useful method of uncovering exactly what a Defendant is worth. It is not uncommon for judgement debtors to misrepresent their circumstances in letters, or even when giving evidence in court. On these occasions, if a Plaintiff is not satisfied with what is being said it is possible to apply for an Oral Examination, which once served on the Defendant results in him having to attend court for the purpose of cross examination. He can also be ordered to produce bank details and anything else that relates to his personal circumstances. Even details of cheque stubs can be examined and the Defendant made to answer questions about his spending habits. In the event a debtor ignores the order to attend court for this examination, it is then possible for the Plaintiff to apply for an Order to have the delinquent debtor committed to prison. Once a claim has reached this stage most Defendants are only too pleased to make an offer of settlement.

For a case to reach the stage of a committal to prison means a considerable period of time has been taken up with attendances at court, making applications and so forth. If during such procedures the Plaintiff has been utilising a firm of solicitors, who in turn could have been instructing barristers, then legal costs could well have reached four or five figures. By self-representation the Plaintiff will have only incurred minimal, bearable costs, which if unrecovered will not leave too large a hole in the pocket.

4   Fraud Investigations

According to the Oxford dictionary, fraud is 'criminal deception; the use of false representations to gain an unjust advantage'. Fraud and other acts of deception occur on a daily basis in most areas of business. Every year millions of pounds go astray into the pockets of highly organised tricksters. Consumers, employees, professionals such as solicitors, company directors and even accountants, are engaging in criminal acts of fraud and various types of deception.

For example, a few years ago a well known banking organisation involved in mortgages hired the services of Eurotec private detectives to investigate a number of suspect mortgage applications. Within a few days it was discovered that several properties had been mortgaged over and over again in different names: in most cases the names and occupations were false and the total loss to the company exceeded two million pounds.

In 1992, another case involved staff employed by a well known music firm, when a finance company was tricked out of £1,200 in the sale of a piano to a Surrey musician. This was a very simple but effective act of deception in that after filling in a credit application for a loan to buy the piano, the sales assistant, without the knowledge of the customer, altered details on the application form in such a way that the musician's general status became more impressive to the loan company. This resulted in the application being accepted and a £1,200 cheque being paid to the music shop, the assistant in turn received commission on the sale.

If it were not for the customer, on receiving his copy of the agreement, noticing that alterations had been made to the application, this deception would never have been uncovered. As soon as he realised he had been presented as the *owner* of his home address instead of a tenant, he contacted the finance company and complained to the managing director. It took only a few hours to discover what had occurred and the salesman was duly dealt with. The musician's alertness and honesty paid dividends: the finance company terminated the agreement and allowed him to keep the piano free of charge.

The above examples are the tip of the fraud iceberg. Other offences involve cheque card applications and general loans for domestic goods, and of course thousands of dud cheques a year are issued to unsuspecting traders. How does one deal with such financial abuse? One can take common sense precautions, and use high-tech gadgets and sophisticated procedures, but unfortunately there is no foolproof way to stop the determined fraudster.

Precautions

A careful and judicious vetting of applications for credit facilities or loans is probably the best method of fooling the trickster. An experienced analyst is worth his or her weight in gold. Such a person can examine a loan application and by instinct alone can tell if the information contained on the form is genuine. If there is any doubt, then they will know instinctively what investigations to activate. However, it is a sad fact of business that such researchers are few and far between. With ever mounting pressure to acquire new business, suppliers and loan company staff are so eager to impress their masters, they can easily be tricked into authorising applications which are in some cases blatantly false.

Example   John Smith has applied for a credit card with a limit of, say £5,000. He has resided at his home address, which is a one bedroom flat, for several years and has a bank account into which his monthly salary is paid by direct debit. Listed on his application are his employers and details of bankers, with account number. Let us imagine that he has held this bank account for three years, and during that time has just about managed to keep his head above water. But because of mounting financial pressures and rent arrears he has decided to acquire the credit card for fraudulent purposes, including the drawing of cash.

All Mr Smith has to do is misrepresent his *tenancy* situation at his home address, by saying he is the *owner* of a semi-detached or terraced house. As long as his name appears on the voters list as being clear of County Court judgements, then further confirmatory enquiries would almost certainly not be made. In fact, on most credit card application forms all the applicant has to do is tick off the section describing himself as a *house owner*, and as long as he is in regular employment a card will be issued. Moreover, employment details can easily be distorted to advantage.

For example, if a person is *self-employed*, or for that matter *unemployed*, all he has to do is create a false employer's name, register with any one of the hundreds of business bureaux offering mail forwarding services and telephone answering facilities, and he can successfully trick anyone into believing he is in full-time employment. This is a very popular method of deceiving consumer loan companies and banks into opening accounts, which then end up losing them thousands of pounds. The files of credit agencies and similar firms are saturated with records of investigations into such cases on the behalf of nationally known organisations who have experienced this kind of deception.

Returning once again to Mr Smith: the moral of the story is simple – no matter how accurate a person's application may *appear* to be, every statement made by the applicant must be checked out. If it is stated he is the owner of a semi-detached house, this had got to be confirmed. Words on an application form are not good evidence, and should be supported by details of any mortgage or other loan charge that might exist on an address. Of course, it is not unusual for a trickster to avoid this precaution by naming himself as the owner without any mortgage, in which case presentation of the property deeds, or a letter from the conveyancing solicitor would be useful back-up evidence. To accept the applicant's word is not good enough.

With respect to *employers*: a simple request for written confirmation of employment would not be unreasonable. For some reason this is very rarely required by firms offering credit or loan facilities. Impressive-looking application forms saturated with information give one the impression that all manner of checks are being carried out. While in some cases this might well be the case, there are thousands of applications for credit a year granted to individuals who are highly organised fraudsters, whose criminality is aided and abetted by the negligence of employees.

Popular Methods of Fraud

It is impossible to describe every method of fraud and deception currently in use. They are so varied and in some cases complex, the fraud investigator has to be an accountant or psychic to uncover the truth. Internal, rather than external, fraud is also a serious problem for many firms: from petty stealing of company funds and cheating on expenses, to directors diverting funds and business into their own pockets.

Employee fraud   By far the most prevalent act of dishonesty is the employee who cheats on expenses. Although petty in character, this kind of dishonesty costs employers millions of pounds a year. Somewhat different to high-tech fraud, this fiddling on expenses can be controlled by the adoption of tighter administrative procedures.

The authorisation for payment of expenses should be vested in one trustworthy individual. All claims should be carefully examined and receipts must be supplied for even the most petty amount of money claimed. There are a few golden rules that should be adhered to in dealing with staff claims for expenses:

- Comprehensive claim forms should be submitted
- Receipts or other vouchers should be attached to claim forms
- All claims must be submitted within a specified time
- If claims are in respect of mileage incurred on private motor vehicles, then total mileage should be declared, along with full addresses visited by the employee

In all employer-staff relationships, it is not uncommon for employees to take their bosses for a ride, especially if it is thought that they can get away with the odd bit of cheating. Therefore the answer is simple: the employer is advised to create a reputation for diligent checking of all expenses. With this kind of security shadowing their activities, staff will be less inclined to steal.

Consumer fraud   In view of the many and varied methods of deceiving suppliers and other firms supplying credit and loan facilities, it is impossible to give specific advice, except to point out that common-sense and diligent checking of all applications should be adopted.

Specially prepared application forms should be used, along with the services of a skilled and tenacious *specialist* who can be trusted to dig deep into an applicant's circumstances. Should the supplying firm not have such a person on staff, then it would be well worthwhile contracting out such work to a suitable member of the Association of British Investigators. A skilled private eye can be an invaluable adjunct to a supplier or finance house. In this day and age most investigators are linked by computer to any number of useful sources and can quickly check the authenticity of any kind of application for credit or loan facilities.

Motor vehicle-related fraud   For many years fraud and deception have been rife in the motor industry. The misrepresentation of car loan applicants by garages and finance brokers, both of whom benefit financially from all accepted credit and hire purchase sales, has been a popular method of cheating for over thirty years.

Small back-street car-traders have been known to actually sell cars to completely bogus customers created by sales staff, all of whom receive commission from sales and introductions to hire purchase companies. The method is so simple that greedy loan companies, anxious to expand their portfolios, have for years been duped into financing vehicles for non-existent customers. On some occasions even the cars did not exist. One bizarre example involved a car, presented with a registration number that turned out to belong to a London bus, which was subjected to several loan deals over the period of a few weeks. The garage introducing the business extracted over a hundred thousand pounds out of the loan company. Fortunately, skilled private investigators were called in to investigate and the perpetrators were finally prosecuted and sentenced to several years in prison.

Whilst precautions have been implemented within the motor finance industry, acts of deception still occur at regular intervals and it is not uncommon for some motor dealers to be party to the fraud. The fact that dealers' staff are in most cases selling on a commission basis will always tempt the more unscrupulous types into cheating. Whilst only occasionally do staff employed by loan companies become involved, it has to be said that negligence, lack of expertise, accompanied by the urge to create new business, assist the criminal planning deception.

On the other hand, garages regularly deceive customers into purchasing unroadworthy vehicles that are often only fit for the scrap heap. Moreover, non mechanically minded customers are paying out millions of pounds a year for repairs that, in some cases, are not really necessary.

Invoicing fraud   All business organisations receive a steady stream of invoices that have to be settled by a certain date. In small firms where there are just a couple of partners or a sole proprietor, cash-flow is much more important than in large, successful firms, and a personal knowledge of what is owed enables partners to identify invoices on arrival.

This is not the case with larger firms, who in a majority of cases receive hundreds of invoices a year for settlement. The task of checking and authorising payments of these bills is usually allocated to a member of staff who has little or no personal knowledge of whether or not the invoices are genuine or correctly calculated. It is true to say that millions of pounds a year must be mistakenly paid to suppliers who are either bogus, or, being genuine, have miscalculated the total amount of an invoice. Banks are notorious for such mistakes, consequently it is reasonable to assume so are other firms.

A 'bogus' invoice is a fraudulently submitted, totally false account that has been sent to a firm in an attempt to deceive. For example, there are currently a number of organised gangs based in Europe sending out false invoices purporting to represent British Telecom phone and fax accounts. These professionally printed documents are headed *IT*, *Tag International Telex* or *Telfax Directories*, with addresses in Zug (Switzerland) or Prague. The amounts displayed are usually between £300 and £400, and in many cases victims have wrongly assumed that these invoices were genuine and have paid up, believing that orders had in fact been placed with the fraudsters. Surrey trading standards investigators are currently looking into these offences, and hopefully the perpetrators will be dealt with in due course.

The most effective precaution for any business which regularly receives invoices is to have some kind of efficient system in operation to confirm first the authenticity of the claimant, and second (if genuine) the amount being claimed. A useful method of keeping track of anticipated invoices is to maintain a simple accounts ledger which shows in alphabetical order details of all orders placed. On receipt of any invoice, by cross-referring to the ledger the authenticity of the account can quickly be established. All this can also be run efficiently on a PC.

Once the status of an account has been verified, it is then prudent to check that the amount is correct. With the aid of the ledger or computer this would only take seconds, assuming comprehensive and accurate information has been recorded.

The consumer must also, of course, be wary of being cheated when receiving bills or invoices. It is essential that the customer carries out basic common-sense checks. For example:

- Is the total of the invoice correct?
- Are the charges justified?
- Are the services or goods recommended really necessary?
- Is the supplier telling the truth with regard to what is being charged, and why?
- If the supplier is an accountant or solicitor, were the hours being billed for actually utilised as described, and has the service been honestly and professionally supplied?

It is imperative to suspect anyone and everyone of making a mistake with calculations or misrepresenting themselves in some manner. Bank and credit card statements in particular should be stringently checked before paying-up. In the event a consumer or business person fails to carry out common-sense checks before parting with money then the victim must carry some of the blame.

Bank and credit card fraud   Credit card frauds are usually pretty basic, and often not very different from standard bank frauds. For example:

(a)   Card holders run up substantial debts never intending to pay them.

(b)   Lost cards are acquired by those who go off on a spending spree and forge the customer's signature.

(c)   From time to time card-holders report cards stolen, when in fact they are still in their possession. Further debts are then incurred.

(d)   Organised gangs of thieves steal credit cards and bank guarantee cards with cheque books.

(e)   Dishonest retail staff note credit card numbers and use them for the telephone purchase of goods and services.

(f)   Dishonest retail staff collude with card-holders to deceive.

There are obvious methods that one can adopt to avoid some of the above situations. The most successful method of protecting a card is for the holder to be security conscious, never engage in credit card purchases over the telephone, and ensure that bank cards and cheque books are not kept together – one is not good without the other. Within the credit card and bank companies there are numerous security systems in operation to protect customers. Unfortunately, well organised thieves regularly bypass these systems and are able to earn themselves millions of pounds a year.

Anyone in business accepting a credit card in payment for goods or services should always request additional forms of identification. A driving licence for example will at least display a name, signature and address. In addition, to utilise the credit card telephone checking system is also essential, bearing in mind the card could have been stolen a short time before, or in other circumstances where the holder is not aware of the loss.

Bank fraud takes many forms and usually involves either customers or staff at various levels. All banks have in place stringent methods for checking on customers; once again, organised thieves do successfully penetrate bank security and make off with thousands of pounds. Bank staff, especially those at a high level, also occasionally go astray and create 'ghost accounts' into which they transfer large amounts of money. However, teams of bank inspectors invariably uncover such frauds and the staff are prosecuted.

Insurance frauds   By far the most successful and difficult-to-detect fraudulent act is insurance claim fraud. Every year thousands of personal accidents, motor accidents, property theft, and such like are the subject of claims to insurance companies. Millions of pounds are paid out to policy-holders who have not been totally honest with their claims.

An example of an easy-to-perpetrate personal accident fraud is the case of R.T.L. (name withheld for legal reasons). This person, living in the north of England alleged serious injuries sustained in an industrial accident, the result of which laid the claimant permanently off work, or so he claimed. The insurance company, unhappy with doctors reports, decided to request private detectives to mount a surveillance on the claimant. After several weeks of watching this person a number of video films were completed, all of which showed that the claimant was fit and well, so much so he was able to engage in long games of golf and squash.

Insurance claims in motor accidents have passed a reasonable level. The annual cost to insurance companies is astronomical and claims are on the increase. The favourite 'trick' of claimants is to persuade garages undertaking insurance accident repairs to exaggerate the accident report that is submitted to the company who, despite sending their own inspector to check things out, are often duped into authorising a repair.

5   Staff Vetting

The selection and employing of staff at any level is a vital aspect of business operations. One wrong decision during the pre-employment phase could result in a disastrous relationship with an employee that causes serious damage to the overall business operation. Even with carefully-checked applicants, it is possible for newly-recruited individuals to change from perfectly efficient members of staff into unreliable, dishonest characters whose conduct causes considerable financial loss.

There are no guarantees when employing and managing staff; the individual's circumstances can change at any time and the first to suffer will almost certainly be the employer. For example, a young woman embarks on the career of her choice, and after a few months suddenly reveals that she is is experiencing difficulties with her husband or boyfriend. More than likely her standard of work will be affected and this in turn will cause inconvenience and financial loss to the employer. There are thousands of such cases a year throughout the country. With fake medical conditions and other unjustifiable absenteeism, staff at all levels are costing employers millions of pounds a year.

How does one avoid inconvenient, costly situations resulting in financial loss to the employer? In all employer-employee relationships it is impossible to *guarantee* the conduct and/or circumstances of a member of staff. Somewhere along the line, niggling or more serious inconveniences will be experienced. And while it is impossible to completely avoid such situations, there are procedures which, if regularly observed will assist the employer in anticipating trouble or keeping such inconveniences to a minimum. These procedures are collectively termed 'positive vetting'.

Positive Vetting

This is a system of checking the claims of an applicant who is being considered for a post which will give him (or her) access to confidential information. Now regularly used in industry, positive vetting can be used for the checking of any kind of individual, from cleaner to senior management level. It is simple, effective, and ideally should be adopted by anyone in the business of pre-employment checks. Once the background of an individual is checked by this method the result is a clear, detailed picture of the applicant.

The system of positive vetting was created by British intelligence agencies and the mandarins of Whitehall, and has been relied upon for many years as a means of security-clearing servicemen, civilian staff and recently certain police officers, who have access to confidential information. When civilian defence companies were working on Ministry contracts, the system was also utilised to check out civilian staff with access to government data. There are numerous defence and other business organisations providing their expertise to the public sector, and all staff working on such projects are the subject of positive vetting.

The security provisions of defence contracts give MI5 the right to inspect all security arrangements, control the placing of sub-contracts and demand full particulars of anyone handling or having access to classified information, or in close contact with such people. MI5 also has the right to order that any person who does not need access to classified information for the proper performance of any contract be excluded from that information. In theory, defence company employees should be vetted like civil servants, which means MoD officers would perform an open but detailed investigation into an individual's personal and political background. The reality is that applicants are vetted secretly by both MI5 and the MoD.

Official security vetting   The procedure works like this. The employee provides comprehensive personal information, such as education details, personal referees, previous addresses and past employers. This information is then passed-on by the employer, via their own security officers or others appointed to deal with a section of MI5 called C2.

The MI5 officer then writes the name of the subject for investigation on a request form and despatches it to the Registry where all MI5 files are kept. If that person is already listed somewhere in MI5's 30 million files, details are passed to F2 section. Officers here search criminal records, via Special Branch and MI5 records, for details of any activity that might warrant restricting access to classified information.

The file is then sent to the C2 branch officer, who classifies the subject in one of four categories. These range from 'A' grade, which allows complete security clearance, down to 'D' grade, which means the employee is not recommended for sensitive work. MI5 passes its report to the MoD security division, which employs about 180 vetting officers. The MoD then decides whether the employee should be allowed to work for the contractor.

The problem with this procedure is that defence contractors rarely argue against the MoD's decision. The fact that certain 'approved' companies rely on MoD contracts as a primary source of business means that it is highly unlikely an employer will argue a case on the behalf of a member of staff declared risky by the authorities. Employees who protest their innocence nevertheless suffer irreparable damage to their professional status.

One such person was Iwan Graves, who in 1985 found his security clearance mysteriously withdrawn from Sciocan, a computer company in Milton Keynes. Informed simply, 'We've got a problem with your clearance under the Official Secrets Act', he was told that his contract was to be terminated. Despite tenacious representation, Graves was unable to penetrate the cloak of secrecy surrounding his vetting. He finally discovered, quite by chance, that he had been recommended for termination not because of what MI5 had discovered about him personally, but because of the political views and activities of one of his relatives.

The secrecy surrounding vetting is so restrictive that even senior officers within defence organisations are often unable to get MI5 to explain certain decisions. MI5 makes companies sign a document known as the 'Secret Aspects Letter' before they take on MoD contracts. This sets out in no uncertain terms the security provisions stipulated by MI5, including its right to check new employees. Defence firms must co-operate, as failure to do so gives the MoD the right to terminate a contract.

The companies themselves are vetted, and organisations allowed access to classified information are placed on a document called 'List X' which contains approximately 2,000 names. MI5 is responsible for the security of the premises and personnel of these companies. Each firm is said to be supplied with a manual which contains guidance on security procedures. Defence firms, security officers and management personnel are encouraged to take special training courses run by officers from C Branch. Some major defence companies carry out their own enquiries into the background of job applicants using private detectives.

However, general confidence in the system has started to decline. There have been a number of cases over recent years where security-cleared individuals have been discovered working as spies for Russian intelligence. One such person, Michael Smith, was employed by a private firm entrusted with Ministry of Defence contracts. Despite working for the KGB for nearly 20 years, Smith's vetting failed to uncover a number of personal characteristics which would have activated warning bells.

The 1993 Old Bailey trial on Smith highlighted apparent inadequacies in security vetting procedures of civilian defence workers. Had it not been for the 1992 defection of KGB Colonel Victor Oschenko, who is said to have recruited Smith in the early 1970s, it is likely that Smith's activities as a KGB spy would never have come to light. Smith, of Burton Road, Kingston-upon-Thames, denied four charges under the Official Secrets Act of collecting and passing-on details of secret weapons to the KGB. The charges related to the year 1990 to 1992, when he was employed by GEC at its Hirst Research Centre in Wembley, but Smith was accused of being a spy for much longer.

After graduating from Surrey University in electronics, Smith joined the Communist Party in the early 1970's and progressed to become secretary of the Kingston branch. It was around that time he was recruited by Oschenko, who was working in London, ostensibly as a diplomat. Despite his communist leanings, Smith managed to procure security clearance, which gave him access to secret information held by Thorn EMI, who employed him on a secret weapons project. Thorn EMI failed to discover during initial vetting that he was a Communist Party official who had attended a Soviet spy-training 'school' in Portugal. As one security source, who cannot be named, said: 'Michael Smith's vetting was too casual.'

Smith's affiliation to the Communist Party eventually came to light, and his security clearance was removed. Smith appealed direct to the then prime minister, Margaret Thatcher, and to the MoD. Shortly afterwards he moved to GEC, where as a quality control manager he was given 'limited' clearance. This lower security grade did not prevent his access to secret material, and in 1990 he was re-activated by the KGB and told to resume his spying operations. Although Smith denied this, it suggested there were flaws in security vetting procedures. The nature of defence industry work is such that all personnel employed by firms entrusted with MoD contracts have to be cleared by both MI5 and the MoD. The companies themselves play little or no part in actual investigations but do liaise with, and act upon the instructions of, the appropriate MI5 or MoD department.

The Michael Smith case is not the first time the efficiency of MI5 has been questioned in court. Hassan Assali, a Libyan electronics expert, had been security-cleared for work on defence projects and worked for a number of defence companies. What MI5 failed to discover during his security vetting was that he was manufacturing bomb-timers for use in the Middle East. Assali, who in 1985 received a nine-year jail sentence for these offences, was also involved with a London security firm connected to MI5 and MI6.

Furthermore, MI5 cannot even be trusted to check its own officers. Several cases of officers selling MI5 records to the Soviets were uncovered in the 1980's, including those of Geoffrey Prime and Michael Bettaney. In such circumstances, it is highly unlikely that the monitoring and checking of the thousands of workers in the defence industry is being carried out successfully. A security source has said: 'Who knows how many spies there are in the defence industry?'

The success of positive vetting relies on the applicant providing a considerable amount of personal information which is submitted on a **PV application form**. As can be seen from the provided example, this form requires so much data it might be necessary for the applicant to use several forms. It is important to ensure that the PV form is completed by the applicant, and not by the employer using information gleaned from a curriculum vitae. The CV, although useful, should not be used to check a potential employee.

Once the PV form is completed, it should then be passed on to someone experienced in carrying out such checks, either a specialist within the firm or, if no such person is available, then an experienced private investigation or recruitment agency will suffice. It is essential to check *every* item of information supplied by the applicant, who ideally should also have provided copies of all documents referred to, i.e. driving licence, passport and birth certificate. It should be remembered that gaps in a person's employment record *can* mean that they have had a spell in prison. During the course of checking the applicant's background, attention should be paid to all addresses supplied by the subject of enquiry; it is essential to confirm that he/she has in fact resided as stated on the dates supplied.

Financial stability   Should a member of staff ever find themselves short of money or financially unstable then it is possible that, if they have access to money or goods, there is a risk that he/she might be tempted to steal from one's employers.

To minimise the risk of this, it would be helpful during the course of positive vetting if credit checks were made against all addresses associated with the subject of enquiry. The procedure for carrying out such investigations is described in chapter one. Any adverse information uncovered from these checks should be carefully considered before coming to any decision about employing the applicant.

Previous employers   The normal method of checking a person's professional track record is to write a letter to the previous

The key to accurate staff vetting is information. Shown below is a recommended style of application form for all new employees which contains the type of information from which accurate vetting can be carried out.

APPLICATION FORM

All information given will be treated as strictly confidential

			OFFICE USE ONLY
POSITION APPLIED FOR	I.T. Systems Manager		
FIRST NAMES & SURNAME	Mr. Simon Meachem		
ADDRESS	42 Carbone Lane New City N17 8OB		
DAYTIME TEL. NO. 484858			
DATE OF BIRTH (AGE) 15.1.55 (40)	PLACE OF BIRTH Bath		
MARITAL STATUS Married	NATIONALITY British		
	SPOUSE'S NAME Anne		
NUMBER OF CHILDREN, NAMES & AGES No children			
PLEASE GIVE DETAILS OF ANY SERIOUS ILLNESSES OR DISABILITIES			OFFICE USE ONLY
NAME & ADDRESS OF YOUR G.P. Dr. Joseph Health Centre, New City	None		
ARE YOU A REGISTERED DISABLED PERSON? No			
NUMBER OF DAYS ILLNESS DURING THE LAST YEAR? 8			
SECONDARY EDUCATION	FROM - TO	EXAMINATIONS & GRADES	OFFICE USE ONLY
New City Secondary School	1966-1971	O' Levels English - A, Maths - A German - A, Science - A	
FURTHER EDUCATION None	FROM - TO	COURSE DETAILS & RESULTS	
PROFESSIONAL QUALIFICATIONS & MEMBERSHIP OF PROFESSIONAL BODIES None			OFFICE USE ONLY
DO YOU HOLD A CURRENT DRIVING LICENCE? YES/NO Yes	Details of any driving convictions during the last 5 years None		

		OFFICE USE ONLY
PASSPORT NUMBER 27659381 DATE OF ISSUE 14/12/94		
PLACE OF ISSUE Staines		
LANGUAGES & SPECIALISED SKILLS German		
BANK : NAME, ADDRESS & A/C No(s). Independent Bank, Station Road, New City		
A.C. No. 007321		
CREDIT CARDS HELD i.e. VISA, ACCESS, etc Visa		

EMPLOYMENT HISTORY
Present or most recent employer first. (Including H.M. Forces)

NAME, ADDRESS & TEL (NATURE OF BUSINESS)	POSITION & MAIN RESPONSIBILITIES	FROM - TO	LEAVING SALARY	REASON FOR LEAVING
New City B.C. High Road New City (Local Government) Tel. 0111-333000	Deputy I.T. Systems Manager Ensuring that all corporate systems & network are running at all times.	1980 - 1995	£80,000	No scope for promotion
HAVE YOU GIVEN NOTICE TO YOUR PRESENT EMPLOYER? YES/NO No		HOW SOON COULD YOU COMMENCE YOUR NEW EMPLOYMENT? 1 month		
PLEASE GIVE DETAILS OF ANY FORTHCOMING HOLIDAY COMMITMENTS None				

PLEASE USE THIS SPACE FOR DETAILS OF INTERESTS/HOBBIES & ANY OTHER INFORMATION YOU CONSIDER RELEVANT. Martial Arts, Chess, Reading	I confirm that the information supplied is accurate.
	Signed : S. Meachem
	Dated : 15.1.95

PLEASE GIVE THE NAMES, ADDRESSES & TEL. NOS. OF TWO REFEREES.	OFFICE USE ONLY
Mr. E. Smithson, Chief Executive. New City B.C. High Road, New City. Tel. 0111-333000	
Dr. Joseph Health Centre. New City Tel. 0111-555822	
DETAILS OF ANY CRIMINAL CONVICTIONS	

employer, who either replies specifically or provides a standard reply. While generally this method can be satisfactory, it is also advisable to contact previous employers by telephone, in order to speak with a member of personnel or management staff who is prepared to provide 'off the record information'.

When carrying out pre-employment checks, it is important to note that suitable written references do not necessarily provide an accurate picture of a person's work history. There are numerous cases where employers, for all manner of legal reasons, have been reluctant to sack staff. Furthermore, people who have been caught with their hand in the till, so to speak, have agreed to resign as long as they are provided with a suitable reference. In other words, the employer is simply adopting the easy way out of his situation by passing the culprit onto another firm.

Criminal records   There has been continuing controversy over the years about access to official files for the purpose of checking criminal records, and whilst certain authorised organisations are allowed access to the Criminal Records files, it is illegal for private organisations and/or individuals to obtain such information.

This is a very frustrating situation for the firm or private businessman who is contemplating the employment of someone who will have access to money or secret business information. Despite the illegality of acquiring criminal records information, there are many private detective agencies and other research organisations who buy and sell such information. However, the Association of British Investigators do not encourage such conduct and any ABI member convicted of such an offence has his membership terminated.

How then does a potential employer confirm that a job applicant does not have a criminal record? The answer is simple: by asking the potential employee to declare details of any criminal convictions on his PV form. The applicant is not only being given the opportunity to come clean, but a situation is also being created whereby the employer can request the applicant to offer proof that he has no criminal convictions. This is done quite legally by the applicant attending his local police station where, for a fee of £10, he/she can obtain details of all information relating to their criminal convictions that are held on computer. In the event there are no convictions on record a suitably worded certificate or letter is provided by the police to the applicant, who in turn can pass it on to the employer.

Staff Irregularities

Despite precautions such as positive vetting, employers will always find themselves in a position of having to investigate the activities of existing staff who are suspected of various types of illegal activity including: petty theft of stock or cash; false claims for expenses; moonlighting for other firms; general breaches of contract; personal use of office facilities; and malingering.

It should be remembered that not only lower-echelon members of a company are prone to illegal conduct. Managers, directors and even partners, can go astray in more serious ways than lower-level staff. Although dealing with such unsavoury characters is always an unpleasant and delicate process, it is not impossible to discreetly investigate their conduct.

Expenses claims   When dealing with false claims for expenses, a casually submitted claim for petrol or other expenses can easily be dealt with by the resident accounts department, who no doubt will have some simple system in operation. However, in the event a member of staff is found to be regularly submitting expenses for a suspected non-visit or occasion, then some kind of surveillance should be activated on the suspect, in which case outside help would be advisable.

In anticipation of staff exaggerating their expense claims, it is always advisable to have very detailed claim forms. Not only will this inhibit employers from even the *thought* of falsifying claims, should it transpire an individual has been tempted a detailed claim form will enable easy checks to be made against what is being presented. The suggested example of a claim form on page 76 shows one method of recording staff expenses.

Moonlighting   This is a popular activity in many areas of business. Shift workers are especially prone to undertaking two, or maybe three, jobs at any one time. Apart from the physical and

STAFF TIME AND EXPENSES REPORT

CLIENT : _____

EMPLOYEE'S NAME : _____ MONTH OF : _____

Date	Commenced	Location	Concluded	Location	DETAILS OF DUTIES	Total Time	Mileage	Misc. Expenses	Operative

mental stress that is experienced from undertaking two or three jobs, working for another organisation engaged in a similar type of work can be counter-productive, and damaging in many ways, to the culprit's primary employer. In any event, the effects of two occupations will eventually take its toll on the individual, the result being that the quality of work all round will decline.

Usually, rumours are the first indication of a moonlighting situation; on some occasions a member of staff will inform on the culprit. In the event the employer is concerned that a member of staff is engaged in work elsewhere, then he/she will probably want to make enquiries. Depending on the gravity of the suspected moonlighting, the employer might just want to approach the employee directly to discuss the matter.

In more serious cases, if the identity of the secondary employer is known, a simple telephone call might elicit the required confirmation. However, it should be remembered that in some occupations 'cash in hand' may well be in operation. Consequently the culprit's name might not be acknowledged to enquirers and under such circumstances further steps will be required.

Surveillance of the suspect will normally result in him/her being successfully followed to the other job. Ideally, investigations of this nature should be left to a surveillance expert. It could well be that a resident security officer is experienced in tailing, in which case the investigation can be handled in-house.

Once it has been confirmed that a member of staff is in fact working elsewhere, then obviously the course of action will have to be considered. Depending on the individual's value to the employer, his/her contact and the seriousness of the transgression, it could well be that dismissal is appropriate.

Theft of stock Despite modern technology and security procedures, organised gangs of staff still manage to successfully get away with millions of pounds a year in stolen stock. In-house security staff not only have their work cut out protecting property, but are known on occasions to be involved themselves in stealing. Industrial firms based at large airports are particularly vulnerable, as are firms on industrial estates.

To investigate internally situations of this nature is very

difficult, and victims are advised to request the services of a reputable security or detective agency, which are very experienced in infiltrating the gangs responsible. Normally, secret investigations are necessary and the employer is sworn to secrecy about such operations. The undercover agent will usually report only to one handler who is a representative of his own company, and under no circumstances will anyone within the client company be aware of the agent's identity. Even management at the highest level should be kept in the dark when such an investigation is underway.

There are numerous examples of cases where, on completion of an undercover assignment of this nature, it is discovered that one of the primary perpetrators is in fact a senior manager, or even a director. It is therefore imperative that every precaution be taken when investigating problems of this nature: trust no-one, not even one's fellow directors or partners.

At the conclusion of an undercover investigation, employers are usually faced with a very delicate situation. It is not unusual for several staff, sometimes managers and even directors, to be exposed as having committed serious criminal offences. Normally, when such people are engaged in unlawful activity, the nature of their offences is very serious, for example industrial espionage or, even worse, sabotage are now becoming common practice in most areas of business.

Every year, hundreds of companies and partnerships lose business secrets to private spies employed by competitors. In some cases senior members of staff, and the occasional director, have been recruited by espionage agents. Other types of business intelligence involves the infiltration of agents into the victim organisation, after which considerable havoc is wreaked by the spy. Secrets are stolen, marketing and development plans for expansion are also usually effected, and even new products and advertising fact-books are often stolen or photographed. The obvious question that arises from such investigations is whether or not to prosecute the offenders.

It is surprising just how many victims have no wish to get involved in a criminal prosecution. Conversely there are some companies, especially in the banking fraternity who generally set an example by instigating criminal charges against all concerned. It is the smaller organisations who tend to shy away from the publicity of a trial, at which they might well experience all manner of embarrassing situations.

External investigations   As we have seen, the most secure, but not necessarily the most economical, method of dealing with a suspected dishonest member of staff, is to enlist the expert services of an outside security or investigation agency. Such organisations, especially members of the ABI, are highly experienced and skilled in covert business investigations, and can offer instant advice. It is also useful to use the services of someone who is not personally connected to a suspect; from the legal perspective, independent expert testimony is always the most valuable. It is also true to say that an outsider is able to maintain a clearer picture, whereas someone who is connected to the suspect will be more susceptible to clouded judgement.

Interviewing techniques   Not all situations call for the expensive expertise of an outside agency (for instance, minor employee transgressions). Streetwise interrogation methods, most of which are currently favoured by police, special branch and the intelligence services, can be an invaluable aid in business situations. For example, during a job interview, if the interviewer can covertly 'interrogate' the applicant, it is likely a more comprehensive character profile will be constructed than if more casual or orthodox methods are adopted.

One interesting (thought ethically questionable) method of screening job applicants utilised by a London-based security company involves recording devices planted in the waiting room. The interviewer, a former police chief, sits in his office listening to the general chit-chat between applicants, and is able to target the suitable applicants long before they have even entered his office. This is a useful method of eliminating candidates who otherwise might slip the net and mislead the potential employer into making a decision that they might regret at a later date.

In the United States there is no doubt about the approach to interviewing and that is: 'The interrogator must be a devious son-of-a-bitch capable of anything to get at the truth.' These are the words of a member of the USAF Office of Special Investigation (OSI).

In any interview situation, be it a simple cross-examination of a member of staff over a minor business problem, a job application, or allegations of misconduct or theft, the interviewer in any or all of the above situations is seeking specific, accurate information: the *truth*.

Human nature is such that in any situation where a person's character, status or credibility is in question, a defence mechanism will automatically switch on, and the individual will adopt a defensive or evasive attitude to the situation. They will probably be untruthful. However, in many cases, the purveyors of untruths are not always aware that they are telling lies; the human brain programmes specific defence mechanisms so that the individual is capable of impressive lies without even realising.

Of course it would be most unfair to accuse everyone in an interview situation of being a liar. Most job applicants, however, are prone to exaggeration of the truth. This is something the potential employer is obliged to consider from the offset of any interview – that the person sitting in the applicant's seat is someone with secrets to hide. It is therefore the job of the interviewer to piece together, by whatever means possible, an accurate character profile of the applicant.

This can be achieved by the following modus operandi (which can apply to job interviews, questioning of staff over general matters, persons suspected of crime, or any other situation in which a business person requires to know the truth of a situation or relationship).

(a)   While many business persons might not like to be referred to as *interrogators*, anyone engaged in the interviewing of another must, if success is to be achieved, accept that they are in fact 'interrogating' and not just having a cosy, informal chat.

(b)   During the course of an interview, it is always useful to have *two* interviewers present, the primary inquisitor being rather more aggressive than his/her colleague. This well-known police method of 'Mr Hard' and 'Mr Soft' can, and regularly does, produce high dividends, especially when the soft individual is introduced as perhaps a trainee member of staff who is on probation and just sitting-in for experience. This scenario tricks the applicant into believing that there is only one interviewer to worry about when in fact Mr Soft is the key player in getting at the truth.

(c) From the moment the applicant enters the room he/she should be observed for tell-tale signs of stress. These include constant flickering of eye lids; dilated eye pupils; muscle spasms in the face; blushing; short, sharp breathing; and rambling or jumpy speech.

(d) At the same time, a visual examination of personal presentation will contribute to a picture of the subject's personality. To an extent, the importance of presentation will depend on the firm's general attitude and atmosphere. So it is up to the interviewers to decide the effect a candidate's dress or hairstyle will have on his/her chances. However, it is generally the case that interviewees who have made the effort to present themselves appropriately are more likely to apply themselves well to the job.

(e) Once introductions have been completed, he/she should be invited to sit in a chair which is so positioned that the secondary interviewer is not in full view; this will create a little unease for the applicant. And in cases where the interview is not a job application but for staff misconduct or suspected theft, the interrogators will have a strong advantage.

(f) During the early stages of the interview it is important to create an ambience of 'There is nothing to fear'; an initial friendly (or so it appears) atmosphere can sometimes pay off. To launch oneself into the 'hard' approach from the offset is not advisable; a gradual probing discussion during which subtle pressure is brought to bear is by far the best method to adopt. It is to be assumed that prior to the arrival of the applicant the interviewer has carried out a general background check of the subject, or for that matter intensive research, which hopefully has led to interesting ammunition that can be used to advantage. For example, one of my own favourite methods is to check the voters list of the applicant and all neighbours, and let it slip in general conversation the names of people listed at the applicant's and neighbours addresses. This invariably tricks the applicant into believing that more is known about him than actually is. To suddenly present details of court judgements for bad debts that have been discovered listed against an applicant can have a very destructive effect on someone who has not been too honest with an application for employment.

My own style of questioning relies mainly on instincts, a sort of sixth sense which tells me when someone is hiding the truth. In the event such a feeling comes over the interviewer, then that is the moment to apply pressure.

(g) After a barrage of hard questioning, it is usual for Mr Hard to leave the interview room under some pretext, with the disorientated subject very unhappy with the course the interview has taken. From this point on, Mr Soft offers the hand of sympathy and friendship to the subject, who is usually only too relieved to open up to a sympathetic ear. This softly, softly approach has been successful time and time again in all manner of situations.

I used it to great effect when a member of my own security staff was suspected of stealing from the offices of a London trading house entrusted to our care. Initial enquiries failed to uncover the culprit who had been stealing from desks and staff wallets. After interviewing all of the client's staff, I was forced to turn my attention to our own security operatives who had been on duty at the time of the thefts. One man's lifestyle was such that he could not possibly afford (on his security pay) to run the large sports car that transported him to work every day.

The plan was simple, with the assistance of City of London police, it was arranged that *all* security officers would attend Wood Street Police Station for an interview, during which a

CID detective would give them a hard time. The suspect, as hoped, became very agitated and when placed in a cell for several hours was a prime candidate for Mr Soft, who turned out to be someone he thought he could trust . . . myself.

The following, which occurred in a police cell, resulted in a confession and successful prosecution.

Mr Soft   Hello mate, how do you feel?

Suspect   Bloody awful, I don't like being branded a thief.

Mr Soft   I know how you must feel, here get this coffee down you, you'll feel better.

Suspect   Thanks a lot – what happens next?

Mr Soft   Well, we've lost the contract and the rest of the blokes are pissed off at you. They really are going to find it hard until they get another job. The trouble is, as freelancers they were relying on this job.

Suspect   Oh shit.

Mr Soft   Why don't you think about telling the truth? At least you will be able to hold your head up high.

Suspect   *does not respond, apart from a sheepish look of guilt.*

Mr Soft   Look mate, I'm here to help you. Tell the truth and I will put in a good word for you. (*Nothing could have been further from the truth.*)

Mr Soft   I don't know if you believe in God, but he is watching over you right at this moment and will continue, as always, to do so. You must tell the truth, for the sake of your mates and your family.

Suspect   I know, but what will happen to me?

Mr Soft   At least you will have told the truth, and we both know what that is, don't we? (*At this stage my voice is very soft and I place my hand gently on the suspect's*

shoulder: physical contact in moments of extreme
stress can work wonders.)

Suspect   *remains silent, but nods his head in the affirmative.*

Mr Soft   What made you take the money?

Suspect   I'm broke and have two ex-wives to support.
             What can you do to help me?

Mr Soft   Look mate, I think we should get a detective in to
             speak with you, tell him the truth and get the
             whole thing off your mind. You'll feel much
             better. I'll see what I can do to help.

Suspect   OK, and thanks a lot for your help and under-
             standing.

A short while later the suspect gave a statement under
caution, admitting to a string of offences, all of stealing
cash from desks and wallets. At a criminal trial in a City
of London Magistrates Court the security operative was
convicted of theft, for which he was given a suspended
six-month jail sentence, he was also ordered to pay costs.

(h) While the soft approach can be a useful aid to interviewing,
    we must not forget Mr Mean – the hard approach can also
    have a dramatic effect on people who are immune to the
    softly, softly approach. A firm, no-nonsense approach to a
    suspect or interviewee might in some incidences be the best
    method of operation. Some people respond more readily to
    a hard-line approach, supported by irrefutable, substan-
    tiated evidence. Threats and/or acts of violence have also
    been known to 'persuade' a person to come clean so to
    speak.
        One such occasion, at Manchester Ringway Airport,
    which is often the subject of much amusement within the
    detective industry, is an incident in which private detectives
    were quizzing suspects employed by a small aviation company
    experiencing thefts from cargo warehouses.
        Unknown to the private eyes, the client, well connected to

American gangsters, was listening-in (on an intercom system) to the questioning of the suspects. Suddenly without a word of warning, the client burst in on the interview of the primary suspect, grabbed him bodily, dragged him out of the chair in which he was sitting next to a large open window, and proceeded to push him out of the seventh storey office. The end result was the suspect being dangled out of the window screaming in terror. The client in turn was shouting obscenities which made it quite clear that in the absence of a confession he was going to drop the suspect onto the concrete below.

This had a dramatic effect, in that the suspect admitted to all manner of criminal offences and named associates also involved, plus the name of receivers responsible for disposing of the stolen items.

Whilst it has to be said such conduct would never be condoned by the author or any other private detective or security operative, the client's method of dealing with the problem certainly did work.

Although I, and other respectable professionals, would never use or condone the use of violence during an interview or interrogation, there is no doubt that violence and other acts of cruelty *do* work.

For example, the most effective cruel, non-violent act is *sleep deprivation*. This is one of the most powerful psychological methods of extracting the truth; it disorientates, saps the will, and leads to an altered state, much like that induced by some drugs. However, push the subject too far and it will not be possible to rely on what they are saying.

The ordeal of Flight Lieutenants John Peters and John Nichol, R.A.F. pilots shot down during the 1991 Gulf War, graphically illustrates the effect of extreme violence. After being captured by the enemy they were transported to *a specialised interrogation unit*, where they were deprived of sleep and then blindfolded, after which they experienced the most horrendous acts of violence.

After several days of this continuing treatment, both officers cracked; however, by then the information extracted was worthless: Nichol reported afterwards that the psychological terror was just as great as the physical torture.

It goes without saying that in a business environment this kind of treatment would not be experienced by job applicants or staff suspected of theft. However, one unusual method of interviewing is by *lie detector*.

In the United States of America the lie detector is much used in law enforcement and business, and the results of such tests are regularly presented in courts of law. In recent years the lie detector has been introduced to England, where it is regularly used in private security and business operations. As yet, the results of a test by this method is not admissible in an English court of law. It is said that Intelligence Vetting Officers at G.C.H.Q. (*Government Communications Headquarters*) are in the habit of using lie detectors in certain situations. If this is true, then it is reasonable to assume that other Intelligence Agencies such as MI5 and the Secret Intelligence Service (MI6) also use this equipment from time to time.

In principal the use of a lie detector in private business is quite acceptable, providing the results are supported with other kinds of corroborative evidence.

The lie detector, otherwise known as the polygraph, although widely used and generally accepted as a sophisticated scientific method of getting at the truth, is deeply flawed.

It relies on the subject finding lying stressful and revealing stress through physiological signals like an increased heart rate, this indication is recorded and observed on a graph-style machine to which the subject is electronically wired.

Despite the usefulness of the polygraph, it is possible for a skilled liar to mislead the detector and to trick the machine into giving a false reading. This is the reason a sensible user of this system will seek corroborative evidence to support the results.

Truth

Getting at the truth is an age old problem that has existed as long as man himself. There are no guarantees when interviewing that the subject is being totally truthful, and in the event the interviewer is in the presence of a skilled no-conscious liar, then there is little or no chance of exposing the subject. Masters of the art of deception have included: *Anthony Blunt*, a former Intelligence Agent-turned-Keeper of the Queen's art collection. Whilst he appeared as a pillar of the arts establishment, he was living a lie, he was in fact a Russian spy.

Publisher *Robert Maxwell* lied his way out of poverty, built an immense business empire out of blatant lies. However, he failed to keep the truth hidden after his death.

A former President of the United States became the incarnation of the lying leader; he denied charges of corruption on live television – two weeks later he was exposed for what he really was.

At the end of the day, a businessman engaged in any kind of interview should rely primarily on *research* into the background of any potential employee. In other words, everything presented by the subject should be thoroughly checked; only then should an applicant be granted an interview. Failure to carry out such checks will almost surely lead to situations of inconvenience or worse.

6   Espionage

For over thirty years in the United Kingdom, private spies have freely gone about their dirty and at times dangerous business. Stealing company information is big business and every year millions of pounds are paid to freelancers and other security firms supposedly providing an orthodox service. In fact many of these individuals and firms are nothing more than industrial spies acting for some of the largest corporate public companies in the country.

Because of the high fees that competitors are willing to pay to industrial spies, there is an ever-expanding proliferation of organisations that offer business intelligence services. These firms are willing to engage in almost any kind of illegal act to steal secret information. Not only will they infiltrate firms, but they regularly install bugging devices, tap telephones, and even steal the contents of rubbish bins. In 1989, a fee of £150,000 was paid in exchange for a single-page document from a pharmaceutical company.

Recent examples of industrial espionage are many. The 1992 case of former Army Captain Jane Turpin, who was recruited to infiltrate a London car parking organisation, is an excellent example of just how far competitors will go to seek out information from the opposition. Miss Turpin did a first class job of infiltrating Euro-Parks by acquiring a job at a high administrative level. Her CV, carefully prepared to trick the victim firm, was so impressive she was readily accepted for the post applied for. This was achieved with little or minimal checking of her credentials and, had the system of Positive Vetting been adhered to, then it is almost certain she would have been uncovered. As it was, she successfully infiltrated Euro-Parks and caused considerable damage.

Her employer was a former senior officer in the Special Air Service turned private spy. For many years, he had operated several security firms and had been engaged in all types of covert spying operations, including the Euro-Parks case, which became the subject of a highly controversial criminal trial at the Old Bailey.

In 1983, the then largest private spying operation ever exposed in Britain involved a former Military Intelligence officer who, working with others with similar backgrounds, organised a long-term surveillance and infiltration of anti-nuclear campaigners protesting at the nuclear power station located at Sizewell in Suffolk. In 1984, one of the campaigners was abducted and murdered. The extent of business espionage is such that more businessmen and women should be aware of the potential of being targeted.

In 1988, the official police magazine *Police Review* considered the general conduct and state of the private spy industry so irregular, it decided to run a series of articles. One report described dealing with the industry very much like encountering the most dangerous jellyfish in the world, the Portuguese man-o'-war. 'It's too nebulous to define its shape or tentacles exactly, but if you touch it . . . by gosh you certainly know it's there.'

On 10 May 1992, yet another exposé in the *Mail on Sunday* revealed that acts of private espionage were being conducted on a scale that no one had so far thought possible. With the assistance of a counter-surveillance specialist and electronic equipment, this newspaper eavesdropped on the streets of London for days, picking up signals from bugging equipment. All manner of private addresses and large firms were isolated as having bugs in their premises.

All those in business should take heed of these warnings, and realise that private spies outnumber official police and intelligence agents. And furthermore there is little legislation to control them.

Information at risk   A wide range of information is of potential interest to spies employed by competitors or by a party which has some interest in a specific firm, perhaps with a view to an aggressive take-over bid or share purchase. In all business organisations there are different types of information at risk:

- Sales figures
- Marketing and advertising plans
- New product information
- Financial data (especially concerning problems in the company)
- Details of clients and contracts
- Personal adverse information relating to staff and directors (which could be used to compromise the company)
- Details of tenders (most useful to competitors who will stoop to anything to win a contract)

Methods of Espionage

Espionage strategies are so varied and numerous it is impossible to report and advise on each and every situation that can occur. However, some methods of stealing company secrets are more common than others. Depending on the client's requirements, it is more than likely that criminal offences will be committed during the operation. Normally, a client does not wish to know of the methods adopted to fulfil requirements. After paying a substantial retainer, the client simply allows the spy to go about his dirty business by whatever method he chooses.

Telephone Tapping and Bugging

Telephone tapping and other forms of bugging office premises are by far the quickest method of acquiring company information. To the lay person, such expressions as 'telephone tapping' and 'bugging' conjure up complicated technical images of electronic wizardry. Put simply, bugging means the use of any form of radio transmitter for the purpose of intercepting conversations in a building or on a telephone line. Transmitters ('bugs') vary in size and can be planted in any room, office, or even a vehicle, and can be installed into a telephone or attached to an actual line. In order to receive the information collected via this method, the spy must listen-in, either personally or with the assistance of a receiver.

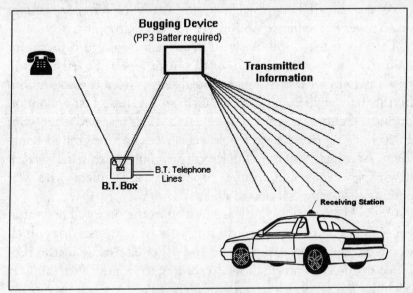

A SIMPLE BUGGING SYSTEM

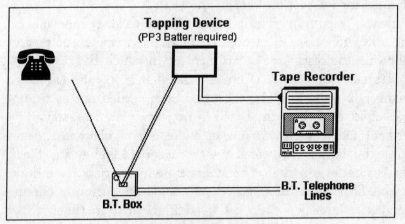

A SIMPLE TELEPHONE TAPPING SYSTEM

An alternative method would be to have secreted somewhere close to the area being monitored an automatic receiver connected to a tape recorder. This was the method adopted by two private detectives in 1988 when they intercepted telephone conversations carried out on the home telephone of a director of Comet. This espionage operation on the behalf of rivals of Comet hit the newspaper headlines, and culminated in a criminal prosecution, during which the trial judge remarked: 'Companies and individuals are entitled to engage in industrial espionage, such as undercover surveillance and electronic eavesdropping.'

This toothless legal position is in effect a green light for industrial spies who, because of the huge fees to be earned, will take any risks for clients eager to steal secrets from the opposition. In the late eighties Professor Michael Beesley of the London Business School claimed his research had revealed that over 2,000 bugging devices were sold each week in the United Kingdom. Another research project carried out by the *Independent* newspaper exposed a former Scotland Yard officer who was offering a bugging service to clients.

On 26 February 1995, it was revealed in the national press that government ministers were hinting at a new privacy law which would outlaw the use of bugging and other electronic methods of collecting private information. According to Home Office minister Nicholas Baker, a new package of planned privacy laws was being planned for ratification later in the year.

He was responding to calls in the Commons for tighter rules on the sale and use of electronic bugging and tapping equipment, following the disclosure of an incident in which Express Newspapers had authorised an electronic surveillance operation against a member of staff. The operation had been carried out by an up-market security company based in London. The firm, staffed by former intelligence officers and such-like, is in regular demand and utilise the most sophisticated devices imaginable. They are able to tap telephones and intercept conversations by a variety of methods.

This firm is one of hundreds of companies currently offering clandestine intelligence services. In addition, there are thousands of freelancers providing similar expertise. And for the DIY enthusiast there are various items of electronic equipment available on the open market that will enable the budding spy to tap into BT telephone lines and cellular phones. Even computers can be monitored and their memory bank and disks drained of confidential information.

As recently as 2 March 1995, Carlton Television's 3D programme conducted a two-day search around London, during which an electronics expert with a special receiving unit intercepted numerous conversations that were being transmitted via bugging devices. Several buildings and firms were identified as having been targeted by industrial spies.

Cellular tapping   The most controversial piece of equipment on the market today is a suitcase monitoring device called **Cellmate**. This illegal but unique gadget is a completely self-contained cellular telephone interception system housed inside a Haliburtan attaché case. It is portable and includes a Panasonic cellular phone, a Marantz professional tape recorder and a 32-Digit (Dual tone Multi Frequency) decoder. Cellmate can be battery or mains powered, and is capable of intercepting specifically targeted cellular phone numbers and recording both sides of the conversation even as they move from cell to cell within the UK cellphone system. This awesome piece of equipment will track pre-programmed numbers and 'lock-on' every time a call is made or received.

Developed in California's Silicon Valley, this equipment is selling rapidly in the UK Even journalists are known to have invested in Cellmate for the purpose of intercepting the conversations of politicians and other high-profile individuals. Private spies are, however, the main users of this equipment, which is very simple to use.

The type of information gleaned from intercepting a person's telephone conversation can be most confidential, as well as potentially compromising. The saga of Princess Diana's illegally bugged telephone calls which were sold to the *Sun* newspaper is evidence of how damaging telephone intercepts can be.

Listening devices   In addition to telephone tapping equipment, there are hundreds of different types of gadgets available on the open market that are 'disguised' bugs. These sophisticated electronic devices are built-in to fountain pens, calculators and other pieces of office equipment, and the victim has little or no idea that conversations are being intercepted. Even British Telecom-style telephone adapters are available that to all intents and purposes appear to be a two-way plug for the BT system: they are in fact powerful radio transmitters.

ROOM/MOBILE TRANSMITTER
POWER SOURCE: lithium battery
PRICE: £240

UXB A robust and serviceable UHF transmitter. Equally suitable for either static use or body worn applications.

ROOM TRANSMITTER
POWER SOURCE: mains
PRICE: £604

UXM Easily concealed 'mains' UHF transmitter. Constant transmission of conversation while connected to the power supply (110–240 volts).

ROOM TRANSMITTER
POWER SOURCE: mains
PRICE: £725

UX-PTM A sub-miniature UHF transmitter has been concealed within a functioning 13-amp adaptor. This highly efficient device is quick to install and blends immediately into its surroundings. A superb piece of electronic engineering.

ROOM TRANSMITTER
POWER SOURCE: mains
PRICE: £750

UX-MK A sub-miniature UHF transmitter housed in an 'exchange' functioning 13-amp twin-switched power outlet. Indistinguishable from the original socket.

PORTABLE TRANSMITTER
POWER SOURCE: watch batteries
PRICE: £630

UXP A standard, fully functional ball-point pen that also conceals a sub-miniature UHF transmitter. A remarkable feat of engineering.

PORTABLE TRANSMITTER
POWER SOURCE: battery
PRICE: £650

UXC 1 A pocket-sized portable calculator that functions in every normal respect. The inbuilt UHF transmitter is totally invisible and highly effective.

ROOM TRANSMITTER
POWER SOURCE: mains/battery
PRICE: £700

UXC 2 A small desk-top version of UXC 1 to be used in circumstances where the larger size is more appropriate.

TELEPHONE TRANSMITTER
POWER SOURCE: telephone line
PRICE: £360

UXT A remarkably powerful UHF telephone transmitter. This series device is easily installed and is suitable for both internal and external use.

UHF RECEIVER 1	**UXR 1** A very sensitive, dedicated two-channel receiver the size of a small cigarette packet.
POWER SOURCE: lithium battery	
PRICE: £450	

UHF RECEIVER 2	**UXR 2** A very sensitive, dedicated three-channel receiver the size of a cigarette packet.
POWER SOURCE: battery	
PRICE: £600	

UHF RECEIVER 3	**UXR 3** A high-gain, long-range receiver with an inbuilt 'carrier activated' automatic tape recorder. Ideal for use in a motor vehicle.
POWER SOURCE: battery	
PRICE: £1,520	

PORTABLE TRANSMITTER	**VXB** Similar in style and application to the UXB, this product operates within the VHF band.
POWER SOURCE: lithium battery	
PRICE: £220	

TELEPHONE TRANSMITTER	**VXT** Similar in style and application to the UXT, this product operates within the VHF band.
POWER SOURCE: telephone line	
PRICE: £285	

VHF RECEIVER	**VXR 1** A very sensitive, dedicated three-channel receiver the size of a cigarette packet. Specifically designed to receive transmissions from VXB and VXT
POWER SOURCE: battery	
PRICE: £295	

INFINITY TRANSMITTER	**INF** A room transmitter that employs the telephone line as the transmission medium. This enables one to listen over any distance, even internationally.
POWER SOURCE: telephone line	
PRICE: £320	

REMOTE SWITCH	**VXS** This is a VHF radio-controlled switching system. The unit comprises a tiny pocket transmitter plus a receiver capable of switching ancillary equipment.
POWER SOURCE: battery	
PRICE: £240	

These impressive listening devices vary in price from the ridiculous to the reasonable, and can be utilised in a variety of disguises. Many are powered by long-life batteries, and others can be wired into the existing electricity system or the power used in BT telephones. The list of bugging devices on pages 94–95 describes but a few of those available on the market today.

The 'Recording Briefcase' The 'Recording Briefcase' has an extraordinary listening and recording capability. Manufactured in high-grade leather and trimmed with good quality brass fittings, the case is totally functional in that there is no false bottom, and therefore no loss of storage capacity. The external dimensions are $17'' \times 12\frac{1}{4}'' \times 4''$ and since the Recording Briefcase is built with discretion in mind, there is no visual evidence, either internally or externally, of its electronic capability.

The briefcase is a purpose-built tool and most of the electronics, including the microphone, are invisibly installed in the case's wooden frame before the leather and linings are applied. Part of the electronic circuitry incorporates a high-powered, self-adjusting amplifier, which guarantees a superb recording, even under adverse conditions. Listening range does of course depend on the ambient background noise. However, in 'boardroom' conditions one would expect to achieve a very satisfactory result over a distance of perhaps 30 feet, with the case closed.

The length of recording time is determined by the type and size of cassette tape employed, the case being designed to accommodate either micro or compact standard cassette equipment (customer's option). The recorder, once installed, is completely concealed, and under normal circumstances even a 'security search' will not reveal its existence. Micro equipment is supplied in its standard format, giving a switchable option on tape speed, while compact standard devices are usually supplied with a reduced motor-speed facility. Maximum recording time (before the tape needs to be 'turned over') is therefore $1\frac{1}{2}$ hours using D120 tapes (compact standard on reduced speed). Recording tapes for both systems are commonly available. When a case is supplied with a recorder, it is usually accompanied with either a D60 or MC60 tape.

The electronic circuits are externally controllable without opening the case, and without any form of visible switching. This of course means that the case may be taken into a meeting 'armed' but not 'active', and recording can be effected at will, and with total discretion. Only high grade components are used in the assembly of this product, and the case is supplied with a year's unconditional guarantee. It is thereafter a fully serviceable instrument.

Personal Surveillance and Infiltration

Infiltration   Some spies will break into and raid an office to copy documents or computer disks. This, however, is very risky and, if time is not crucial, it is more usual for a spy to infiltrate the target firm by obtaining a job. This could mean applying for a full-time post as one of the firm's operating staff, which is a complex ruse.

An alternative method of infiltration is for the spy to sell his services as a *cleaner*. This will allow the spy to operate out of normal office hours. Remember that cleaners will have access to all areas of an office, and to casually photocopy or steal documents would be very easy for a spy posing as a cleaner. A truly professional espionage agent engaged on a long-term spy mission will even go to the trouble of enrolling with a cleaning company for the purpose of gaining access to the target premises.

Another highly successful method of acquiring company information is to approach the victim as a client, and even actually engage in a business transaction. Not many firms will suspect a customer; most businessmen/women, on the brink of a good deal, will impart information without thinking that the new client could in fact be a highly experienced industrial spy. Posing as a client is one of the best methods the spy can adopt; it will invariably result in access to the target's office premises and a personal relationship developing between the respective individuals. In the event the spy is an attractive female, then the victim company is almost certainly doomed.

Personal Surveillance   This is a safe and more or less legal method of stealing company information. All the spy has to do is identify individuals known to be employed by the victim firm. By eavesdropping on general conversations, say during lunch at the local pub or restaurant used by staff, it is surprising what will be overheard. Frustrated employees are only too keen to discuss business and their gripes, which invariably will include topics they should not be discussing. There are a number of Surrey restaurants known to be used by defence company executives and government agency staff, who are in the habit of heavy drinking and loudly discussing secret topics. It is not uncommon for the casual listener to overhear mention of CIA and FBI matters at these establishments. Even MI5, MI6 and Special Branch officers are prone to loose chit-chat.

In all cases where the industrial spy is resorting to the eaves-droppping method, a miniature tape recorder will be in operation either body-worn or installed in a briefcase, handbag or purse. All male employees employed on confidential work should beware of attractive females who make a point of engaging in conversation. Young women make excellent spies, and in some cases they are prepared to go to any lengths to steal information.

In 1984 a notorious business private detective renowned for his expertise as an industrial spy, offered the services of homosexual undercover agents to a client seeking to investigate members of staff suspected of selling company secrets. In a conversation that was tape recorded, the detective agreed to arrange for the gay agents to seduce members of staff who were also said to be gay. What this sleazy detective did not know, was that the 'client' was an undercover investigator from Eurotec private investigators of London, collecting evidence of the detective's criminal activities on the behalf of a national newspaper.

Counter-surveillance

The first and most important weapons to employ against espionage are common-sense precautions.

Precautionary Measures

There follows a list of basic procedures which can foil attempted espionage.

- Vet all staff prior to employment
- Carefully check out all new clients before accepting their business
- Do not become a slave to telecommunications, especially cellular, when discussing confidential business matters
- Remember, all telephone equipment is vulnerable and can easily be intercepted – including fax transmissions
- Ensure that confidential business information is only released to staff who *need to know*
- Never reveal the location of confidential meetings. Wait until the last moment before announcing the venue. In the event an ultra-secret meeting is being held, the venue should not be released to *anyone*. Those attending can be transported from a central point
- Never leave sensitive company documents lying around the office. All such paperwork should be kept in secure locked cabinets
- Ensure that all waste bins and garbage containers do not contain copies or spare documents. Ideally, all such paper should be shredded
- Any external cleaning companies employed should be carefully vetted

The importance of one of these defence mechanisms cannot be overemphasised: **control the imparting of information on all telephones.** At first this may sound a very difficult task but this is not so. By applying common sense and substituting **code words** for product names or sales titles, telephone conversations can easily be orchestrated to confuse an eavesdropper. Dates and venues of important meetings should *never* be mentioned during telephone conversations, and memos prepared for such occasions should always be circulated to only those who *need to know*, after which they should either be destroyed or kept in a secure area.

All telephone conversations should be conducted on the assumption that someone, somewhere could be listening-in. Staff with knowledge of confidential company business should be briefed and made to realise that loose talk can cause serious damage, and ultimately result in loss of jobs. Ideally, all staff should be tied to contracts which contain a confidentiality clause and specific mention of security of information.

The 'Need to Know' principle Business competitors have a continuing lust for information, and some will go to any lengths to steal company secrets. Generally speaking, the task of acquiring a rival's confidential data is often made very easy by the lack of common sense and control exercised by some firms. Loose talk is by far the worst breach of security regularly committed in business today. Members of staff, including managers and, on occasions, directors are prone to releasing information to people who have no need to know.

For example, what is the point of a clerk or bookkeeper in accounts having information about a new product launch or a new contract being negotiated by management? Allowing such staff access to this kind of information is tantamount to sending an invitation to the competition. Much is said about 'the competition' without really appreciating fully who and what the *competition* really is: *anyone* in the same or similar line of business.

Employees should only be allowed access to that information required by them to complete their own task within the company. In some cases there will be an overlap with information, in which case **security briefings** should be held on a regular basis, and all staff impressed to keep their lips sealed when out of the office. Casual chats in pubs and coffee bars should exclude mention of any confidential business information.

This principle should also be applied to clients who more often than not will be inquisitive about what is going on within a firm they are considering employing. To outsiders especially, *only* impart information on a 'need to know' basis.

If, despite taking these precautions, a firm suspects that some sort of surveillance is in operation then it must obviously take steps to investigate.

Discovering and Disrupting Surveillance

There are no official or standard methods of dealing with industrial spies. Counter-espionage is very much a 'try it and see' activity that can, and does on occasion, go very wrong. Training courses for such problems do not exist. Government agencies such as MI5 use 'on the job' training, with highly experienced, former field operatives acting as instructors, to ensure that basic ground rules and systems are adopted.

The following describes a general course of action which should reveal a surveillance operation.

1. Should anyone in business suspect that they are the victim of private espionage, it is in their interests to seek outside expert assistance. And until such services have been obtained it is essential that nothing is said or done within the company to reveal that suspicions have been aroused. For example, to use a company telephone to discuss one's worries would be very unwise, especially by telephoning a security firm. Once there is any hint of espionage, it should be assumed that all telephone calls are being monitored. Furthermore, the possibility of an employee being on the payroll of those responsible should also be considered highly likely.

    Any victim of industrial espionage should think carefully before attempting to deal with the problem internally. Modern spies are devious and capable of ingenious tricks to seek out confidential business information. In addition to these personal skills, they also have at their disposal high-tech electronic equipment with which they can intercept telephone conversations, car-phone communications, and any discussion being held in private or business premises. It should also be remembered that modern surveillance equipment can be remotely controlled and the actual spy can be many miles from the scene (as with the 'Infinity Transmitter' for instance).

    Counter-intelligence security firms have access to sophisticated electronic de-bugging equipment, and in a matter of hours should be able to detect and locate bugs or any other espionage gadget that is in operation. If the victim should prefer to purchase de-bugging equipment for personal use then this can be done; however, be warned, it requires great skill to operate and success depends primarily on the ability of the operator to interpret and understand signals received on the de-bugging equipment. The best counter-surveillance experts are invariably former spies who have 'switched sides'.

2. If the firm decides it must take immediate and independent

action, a thorough physical search should be carried out, with particular attention being given to all telephones and offices where confidential information is housed. Telephone junction boxes should be examined for anything out of the ordinary, as well as the main switchboard. Directors' offices should also be searched for bugging devices: underneath desks and behind wall pictures or curtains are some of the preferred places to plant a bug. The search should be as discreet as possible (at evening or on weekends).

The trouble with an internal search of this nature is that the average person will not know what they are looking for. Transmitters are often minute and installed in office equipment or plugs that are quite genuine and functional, so that even electronics experts have difficulty in discovering where they are planted. Even telecom engineers can be fooled by sophisticated tapping devices.

For potential victims who wish to carry out electronic checks for bugging devices, there are numerous pieces of equipment that can be purchased at varying prices. Simple-to-use hand-held detectors are quite useful at locating bugs that are in operation. The more complicated 'Spectrum Analyser' which is designed to test telephone communications systems, is probably the most all-encompassing counter surveillance tool available. While much of the counter-surveillance equipment available today can be useful, there are occasions when such expensive tools fail to detect breaches of security.

Moreover, in some cases such equipment is very expensive (in excess of £3,000) and can be very difficult to use. To complicate matters further, the eavesdropping equipment currently being used by industrial spies is so sophisticated it is possible for skilled operators with expensive kit to be fooled by expertly installed electronic surveillance gadgets.

3. If the company knows from general circumstances that there has been a leak of information, a list of staff with access to that information should be prepared. All staff included on this list should be considered suspect until such time they are cleared of any wrong-doing.

Once the list is prepared then all those named should be investigated, with particular attention being paid to any contact they may have had with competitors, either by way of previous employment or socialising. Motives should also be considered. Any member of staff who is discovered to have financial, domestic or drink problems should be highlighted for special investigation. Recent unusual incidents or circumstances involving anyone listed could also be a warning sign. These could include:

- Periods of sickness resulting in absence
- Requests for a pay rise that have been refused
- Extra-marital affairs with another member of staff or an outsider
- Continuous non-business telephone conversations

4. If nothing is found inside the building, then it is advisable to examine the whole area surrounding the premises. Attention should be directed to all telephone lines and junctions, as well as office windows, ledges and such-like. If any kind of car or van is frequently parked in direct view of the building, it would be advisable to note details of the vehicle and any occupants. Apparently empty vehicles, especially a commercial van showing some kind of radio aerial, are especially suspect.

If a major espionage operation has been mounted, then consideration should be given to the possibility that the perpetrators have gone to the trouble and expense of acquiring private premises close to the victim. This is a popular method of receiving conversations transmitted via electronic listening devices. It should be remembered that industrial spies will go to extraordinary lengths to steal certain kinds of business information. One just has to remember the recent British Airways spying scandal directed against Virgin Airlines to appreciate what large organisations are capable of. In such cases, electronic listening devices are usually used and the services of freelance spies are invariably enlisted.

The clearest way to explain a good strategy for dealing with espionage is to recount in detail a real-life, successful operation.

An Exemplary Tale

On 2 February 1991, the managing director of a London-based export company was engaged in a telephone call to one of his major clients and at the conclusion of the conversation he replaced the telephone receiver. Within seconds he picked up the telephone handset intending to dial another client. Much to his surprise, he discovered that someone else was speaking on the line. In view of the fact this was an ex-directory personal telephone installation, he decided to listen-in to the conversation.

What was overheard shocked the MD. Every detail of his last conversation was being discussed by a man and woman, who had obviously been eavesdropping on the whole of the discussion with the important client. Details of an overseas contract, costs and other confidential matters were all being enthusiastically thrashed out by the eavesdroppers. One thing that worried the MD more than anything was something the female eavesdropper said to her associate: 'Have we got it all on tape?' The man replied, 'Yup, that makes six cassettes in all.'

Replacing the receiver, the MD adopted a sensible course of action. He immediately left his office and called upon his business partner, someone he knew he could trust, and suggested they go out for a coffee. He revealed to his partner what he had experienced. It transpired that the partner had also experienced 'funny noises' on his office telephone, and that his home telephone had also been 'acting up'.

Being aware that, as a recently-formed export company, they had possibly ruffled the feathers of the competition, the partners came to the conclusion that someone was attempting to obtain details of their clients and prices by tapping their telephones. Little did the partners realise that they would eventually uncover a massive espionage operation that had been ordered by a disgruntled competitor.

The partners travelled by taxi to the offices of a London solicitor experienced in company affairs and litigation. So far *no* discussion had been held on the target premises and, as was to be discovered at a later date, this precaution was a major contribution to tracking down the spies. The solicitor's immediate advice was to recommend the services of a detective agency known to the law firm. Within an hour the Principal of the detective firm was present at the discussion. After hearing the complaints of the partners, the detective advised them to return to work and act *as normal*, and under no circumstances to discuss the problem with any member of staff.

It was also suggested that for the time being all telephone calls of a confidential nature should be aborted. The detective also arranged with the partners to enter the premises after work hours that evening. Fortunately, the tapped telephone discovery occurred on the Friday of a Bank Holiday weekend, which meant that the whole weekend could be used to advantage.

One method of searching for electronic surveillance devices is known in the spy fraternity as 'sweeping', and this is what took place through the weekend. Assisted by two experts armed with specialist counter-surveillance equipment, the private detective carried out a thorough search of the whole of the export company's offices. At the conclusion of the search a plethora of electronic gadgets was uncovered.

In the MD's office, an infinity-type transmitter was found in the handset of the telephone. A two-way 13-amp adapter plugged into the wall was in fact a bug with a remote on/off facility. The range was later confirmed as being approximately two miles.

In the partner's office, a similar device was discovered in the telephone handset. Although there was no twin adapter, there was a very powerful transmitter (again with an on/off remote facility) implanted inside a large pot holding a yucca plant. In the sales office, where important client information was held, was a transmitter built into a calculator, and an unusual telephone tap on the small BT switchboard jointly used by a receptionist, three sales staff, and a bookkeeper.

By late Saturday afternoon, a clear picture of electronic eavesdropping had emerged and the partners were faced with a worrying situation. Their initial reaction was to call in the police. However, in view of possible embarrassment to clients it was decided to investigate further and to find out who was responsible, before deciding on what course of action to take.

After consultation with investigators, it was decided to carry out a search of staff working areas, desks and such-like. This was a wise move: in the desk of a sales representative was discovered a filo-fax in which was found the business card of a rival company. On the reverse of the card was the home telephone number of the company security officer who, it later transpired, was a former Military Intelligence officer.

The rival firm was a large organisation based at Gatwick Airport which, following the formation of the victim's smaller export company, had lost several clients to the partners' more personal and efficient service. The sales rep in whose filo-fax the card had been found was a former employee of the rival company, or so the partners had been led to believe. The discovery of the filo-fax immediately directed suspicion on the sales representative. Accordingly, several special investigators were called to the offices of the victim company and throughout the Sunday a general counter-espionage plan was conceived.

The first move was to examine the personal file of the sales representative. This was not particularly useful because the partners had not done any real checks on the rep (see chapter five) at the time he applied for the job. On the basis of a simple, impressive, written reference which stated that the employee wished to move house to London, this being the reason for a change of employment, the partners had signed him up on a six-month probationary period as a sales representative.

No formal application had been completed, and previous employers had never been declared. The partners had (wrongly) assumed that the man was honest and that the larger, more established firm had done their own homework, therefore he must have been alright. Nothing could have been further from the truth. This man was not in fact an ex-employee of the rival firm, but an experienced undercover spy employed by a London company who had, for several years, provided a secret spy service to the rival firm, via the security officer.

Armed only with the information from the rep's file the detectives could only suggest that he would have to be investigated. This was duly organised, and for several days a surveillance team monitored his every move. The electronic devices in the meantime were left in place.

During the week of monitoring the rep's activities, a search was also carried out of the partner's homes where, not surprisingly, devices were also discovered on the telephones. The perpetrators had obtained details of the partners' private addresses from the publicly available company records stored in the London branch of Companies House. The rest had been easy: during a weekend when the partners and their families had been away on a holiday, the spies had broken into the houses and planted the bugging devices.

As far as the office was concerned, the bogus sales representative had obtained copies of the office keys and arranged for his fellow conspirators to have easy access to the building. According to the rival firm's instructions, the spies were to obtain details of the partners' client list, along with other potential clients being canvassed. In addition, expansion and sales plans had also been requested. An interest had also been shown in the relationship between the partners and clients. In particular the rivals were keen to discover if the partners were very friendly with specific members of staff within client organisations. A more sinister aspect of the operation was a request for details of any criminal offences that might have been registered against the partners and their employees. Furthermore, information of any unusual sexual practices had also been requested.

It was not until Thursday morning of that week that the rep was seen, in clandestine circumstances, in a London hotel foyer where he furtively handed documents to a female, who immediately departed the building. She in turn was tailed to offices in the Cheapside area of the City, where she entered an office block protected by an electronic intercom system. A sign on the door displayed the name of a security firm known to have connections with the security services. It took only a few hours for Eurotec operatives to compile a dossier on this firm. They were silled in the art of telephone tapping and other forms of electronic surveillance. A visit to a nearby underground car park associated with the office block meant that investigators were able to identify all of the covert surveillance vehicles in use by the spy agency. One particular vehicle, a small motorised caravan, turned out to be a mobile eavesdropping centre utilised for receiving transmitted conversations via bugs and telephone taps. Two days later this vehicle was seen parked close to the victim's premises.

Within a few hours of tailing the representative to the security firm's contact, a meeting was convened between detectives and the victims. For obvious reasons, this discussion was held outside of London and in an area that was convenient to observe by back-up investigators, whose job was to confirm that the victims themselves were not under any kind of surveillance. In a room that had been swept for electronic listening devices, a plan was hatched to deal with the industrial spies: the idea was to engage the culprits in a 'sting' operation.

The plan prepared by investigators was that a bogus potential new client would telephone the victim's firm, enquiring about utilising their services. A long telephone discussion would be held, during which a potentially lucrative deal would be discussed and a meeting arranged at an office at Heathrow Airport.

The object of this exercise was to ensure that the eavesdroppers listening into the conversation would receive what they believed to be information of great interest to the rival firm. The address at Heathrow was an existing large freight firm which had agreed to the installation of a special telephone number registered in the name of the bogus firm. The scene was perfectly set: the spies simply had to intercept the telephone conversation and contact their clients.

Everything went according to plan, with the bogus client contacting the victim's firm. The caller was actually the chief of investigations from the detective agency. During the conversation, observations were kept in the street close to the victim's office and sure enough, a motorised caravan from the spies' HQ was spotted parked very close to the building. On the roof was a long radio receiver aerial.

Eventually, the conversation was terminated and a meeting at Heathrow arranged for three days hence. What the spies did not know was that their mobile listening post was filmed. Also a listening device had been placed inside the caravan and everything that was discussed, including a cellular telephone call to their headquarters, was tape recorded. During the three days, a private operative was on duty during normal working hours at the Heathrow office, the assumption being that a member of the rival firm would make contact with a view to stealing the potential new contract.

Sure enough, within 48 hours a call was received (and tape

recorded) from a sweet-talking female representing the rival firm, who insisted that they could provide a more efficient and cheaper service than any other export firm in the country. Without directly questioning the caller, the detective arranged for the woman and her MD to attend the office for a meeting about the possibility of utilising their services.

Two hours later, the woman and her boss – the individual who had initially activated the espionage operation on the smaller firm – attended Heathrow, where carefully prepared signs and scenes had been set. In a room where two secretly installed tape recorders were in operation, private detectives presented themselves as an export firm seeking the services of a reputable agent. In the conversation that followed, the rivals were carefully coaxed into believing that they had every chance of procuring the contract. At a suitable stage of discussion, it was announced by one of the detectives: 'I think it is only fair to tell you that we have had an offer from a smaller firm who sound as though they will be able to represent us as required.'

This brief statement resulted in an outburst from the visiting pair which is still talked about today. The female, aided by her boss, who incidentally had already quoted figures well below that discussed in the 'sting' telephone call, proceeded to slander the smaller firm with false allegations of inefficiency and untruths about the partners being convicted criminals. When cross examined by the detectives as to how they knew this to be so, they actually boasted that they had paid a security firm to infiltrate their competitors.

Having reached a stage where it was considered that sufficient evidence had been obtained, the operative in charge of the 'sting' excused himself, and left the room. A few minutes later he returned, accompanied by three people – the partners of the victim firm and a well-known criminal lawyer. After a few moments of silence, the investigation chief introduced the solicitor and said: 'And of course you know these two gentlemen only too well.'

Over a period of 45 minutes, it was explained to the rival firm's MD that the partners had been aware of the illegal surveillance that had been taking place and that unless certain undertakings were guaranteed, then litigation would most certainly be activated against the rival firm and its directors. Mention was also made of criminal proceedings.

After examining a video of the security firm's mobile receiving caravan and film of the sales representative handing over documents stolen from the partnership, the two culprits actually attempted to deny any involvement in the espionage operation. They attempted to bluff their way out of the office. However, after hearing the tape recording of their bragging admission made earlier during the meeting, they eventually conceded that perhaps they had been a little over-zealous with regard to the competition created by the new partnership. Not wishing to get involved in any kind of public examination of the situation, the MD was only too happy to enter into an agreement with the lawyer.

The general terms were as follows:

- The rival firm would instruct their security agents to cease surveillance and remove all telephone taps and bugging devices from the office premises and the homes of the partners
- The rival firm would give an undertaking not to engage in any similar surveillance in the future
- No attempt would be made to procure, trick, or in any way subvert clients of the partnership
- The rival firm would be responsible for all of the partnership's costs incurred as a result of instructing solicitors and private investigators

The above undertakings were part of a very lengthy agreement that was eventually signed in the presence of all concerned, including the former Military Intelligence officer in charge of the security firm responsible for the espionage operation. This was not a low-key exercise, this was a full-blown espionage project hell-bent on sabotaging the partners' small company. It was a typical example of the larger, more powerful outfit attempting to destroy the smaller enterprise. In exchange for their espionage expertise, the spies had been paid a retainer of £20,000, with a promise of a further £150,000 on completion.

The partners of the smaller firm were very lucky in that from the offset they took every sensible course of action. So much so they were able to quickly round-up the culprits and reach an agreement, which in the end resulted in all of their costs being honoured by those responsible. The experience served to alert the partners into appreciating that in order to survive in business one had to be wary of the dirty tricks capability of competitors.

Throughout the following months the partners regularly called upon experts to electronically sweep their offices and homes for listening devices, especially on occasions when confidential meetings were in the offing. Tape recorders are now standard practice on all business and domestic telephones, and the partners keep a regular check on any strangers calling to the office. Staff are expected to clean the office themselves, and the services of contract cleaners have not been entertained.

The partnership is now a flourishing concern, employing many more staff than at the time of this unfortunate experience. New employees include a security investigator (a retired police officer) whose job is to vet all applicants, monitor the activities of staff, and check on everyone connected to or associated with the firm. In addition, he keeps in regular contact with clients to ensure that they are satisfied with the partnership's services, and behind the scenes he monitors the creditworthiness and general financial stability of clients. He also liaises with credit reference agencies and, when required, employs the freelance services of outside investigators and security consultants who from time to time undertake surveillance and checking of staff suspected of false expense claims and such-like.

7 Office and Technological Security

Security of Premises

Modern office blocks are usually reasonably secure. However, there are still many older buildings where security is virtually non-existent; so much so that brazen thieves are able to walk in from the street, steal items of equipment and walk away unchallenged. If the unrehearsed thief is able to do this, then the experienced industrial spy will have no problem in gaining access to an office. Increasingly, insurance companies are insisting on tighter security for businesses. The following checklist should be useful.

1. **Access**   Common sense should prevail, with some kind of access control in force. Ideally, a security receptionist should be employed to receive all callers who, after proving their identity, should be escorted to a suitable hospitality room where a meeting can be conducted. Wherever possible, visitors should not be allowed access to operational areas of a business organisation, and where possible a special room should be set aside for all meetings. By allowing visitors (even clients) the freedom of the office, one is creating a potential breach of security.

2. **Doors**   The weakest part of any building is quite often the door. All entrances should be protected by solid doors with secure frames and security locks. Hinges should have their screw heads burred to prevent removal. If valuable items such as computer disks and documents containing important information are kept

in the building, then consideration should be given to fire doors. An alternative type of door that improves security is the roller/shutter entrance protector. Glass doors are *not* recommended.

3. **Windows**   Without doubt, the easiest point of entry for the budding thief is a window. All such points of entry should be securely installed and made of reinforced glass; security locks are available for fitting to most styles of windows.

4. **Alarms**   To ensure optimum security, it would be advisable to have alarms (connected to a local police station or security centre) fitted to all access points of the office. It is also advisable to install a suitable alarm within the office, which once again could be connected to a security centre or the local police.

5. **Lighting**   External and internal security lights should be in operation during hours of darkness.

6. **Locks**   There are numerous types of lock, each with its particular function. It is essential to good security that the *right type* of locks are installed at various points on business premises.

7. **CCTV**   Closed circuit television is an invaluable security aid. A major benefit is that cameras do seem to deter criminals from attempting to enter premises. A CCTV system includes small, discreet, sometimes covert, cameras positioned at suitable positions around the building. The cameras are connected to a base station which includes a video machine operating during the hours of darkness. Assisted by suitable security lights, the cameras are able to record all activity inside or outside of the office.

8. **Approach alarms**   A cheap and simple but useful device. Via an adjustable beam, which is transmitted from a small sensor positioned overlooking the area of potential access, this gadget automatically sets off an audio alarm. It can also be used *inside* the premises, and is an excellent early warning system for anyone inside the building working alone or guarding the building at night.

9. **Peepholes**   Security peepholes are nothing more than small lenses arranged to provide magnified wide-angle vision. They can

be installed in doors, in walls or partitions, and are a simple method of confirming who is outside a door before opening up.

10. **Intercom systems** Most modern office buildings have such systems in operation. Comprising of a buzzer and speak-phone, visitors can be questioned before being allowed access to a building.

11. **Deterrent signs** It is surprising the effect that signs can have on an individual about to break into a building. For example 'Beware of the Dog' is a simple but effective method of changing the thief's mind. There are many different signs in use today, and most of them are quite effective. Anyone contemplating the use of such security precautions can have a sign tailor-made to their own requirements. The following are just a few examples:

WARNING STORE DETECTIVES ON PATROL

WARNING – GUARD DOGS

WE PROSECUTE ALL SHOPLIFTERS

CCTV IN OPERATION

NUCLEAR WASTE STORED ON PREMISES

PLAIN CLOTHES SECURITY OFFICERS ON DUTY

DANGEROUS ANIMALS ON SITE

12. **Perimeter fences** For the business operating in a com-pound or large industrial area, a perimeter fence and gate can inhibit, but certainly not prevent, a potential intruder. However, if gates and fences are alarmed and/or protected by early warning systems, then the intruder's job is made far more difficult. The best deterrent of course is a couple of well trained and vicious guard dogs patrolling the area after work hours. In addition, if an alert night-guard was positioned at a strategic point overlooking all points of possible entry, then this would increase security to such an extent that even the most determined criminal would think twice before attempting to break in.

Document and Computer Security

It is surprising just how many business premises are littered with confidential documents and computer disks. Even during the normal working hours, outsiders who are not always known to staff are allowed to wander around unchallenged. Who is to know that such people are not casual thieves, or for that matter industrial spies checking out security with a view to installing bugs?

It is an integral part of protecting information that all confidential documents and computer disks are kept out of sight of visitors. Even computer screens showing data, especially code words, should be restricted to staff only. This is why (as already recommended) all visitors should be escorted to a special hospitality room to conduct their business.

At the conclusion of business each day, a member of staff (appointed say on a weekly or monthly basis) should be charged with ensuring that all confidential documents and computer disks are secured in a locked cabinet or safe. Trash bins should also be emptied, *not* into an outside container but into an incinerator or shredder. If this is not possible, waste disposal units which are difficult to 'get in' should be available.

In the case of staff, it is essential that no member is allowed access to confidential information unless they have been carefully checked out. The 'need to know' principle should always be applied in cases where staff are being appointed to lock-up confidential papers and/or computer disks. Some employers might well be better off ensuring that all staff are responsible for the safe keeping of their own workload.

Protection against 'Techno-bandits'   The criminal art of hacking into computer databases to steal information, or for the purpose of sabotaging stored files, is so refined that Scotland Yard now have a special computer investigation squad whose officers are experts in this field. Increasingly, *no* computer files are safe. Skilful hackers, some very young, are capable of by-passing sophisticated security systems and getting into secret files. Once they have gained access they can then download whatever information they require, or wreak havoc by turning a virus loose into the system.

On a slightly different front, organised gangs of thieves are targeting London firms, duping their way into offices and stripping computer systems of memory chips. Many of these chips are manufactured in Japan and, in the aftermath of the recent earthquake which devastated the city of Kobe, have become difficult to acquire. At midnight on 7 March 1995, such a gang gained access to the offices of accountants Touche Ross by claiming to be emergency air-conditioning engineers. Within hours, they had stripped a series of personal computers of thousands of pounds-worth of memory chips.

At another London address, the imposing Victoria House in Holborn, thieves removed memory boards from computer equipment, and then went on to raid numerous other offices including Victoria Insurance, British Telecom, Sun Life of Canada and the Automobile Association.

According to City of London police, there are three or four professional gangs touring the country, their primary target being computer memory chips because of their rising value. A recent Treasury memo to all government departments and agencies warned of this growing problem.

The only protection that businesses can adopt to protect their computer equipment is common-sense security of the premises. Deny office access to unauthorised persons and all will be safe. On the other hand, security of data from skilled hackers is a much more difficult problem.

In any computer database there are specific files that can only be accessed with a code name or password. Once the hacker knows the password he is home and dry. It therefore makes good sense to restrict the password to only staff who need to know such information. Under no circumstances should there be office memos lying around with computer passwords displayed for all to view.

There have been a number of recent cases involving commercial firms, government and military organisations, where hackers have penetrated top secret files. In one such case a NATO computer system was targeted by a schoolboy computer wizard, who also accessed a number of sensitive intelligence systems.

In addition to restricting password information, it is also essential to regularly change passwords on a weekly or monthly basis. An additional precaution would be to copy all files onto back-up disks, and store such copies at a separate location. This will reduce inconvenience to a minimum should data be lost or stolen.

In companies where there are several computers working as a network, linking different departments, it is essential that one person be appointed as **supervisor**, whose duties should include security control of passwords. In the event certain staff are allocated duties that entail access to files, then some sort of multi-password system should be adopted, so that each person has access only to those files he/she needs.

8 Surveillance and Personal Protection

In today's fast-moving environment, surveillance and personal protection are accepted by some firms as being a regular feature of everyday business operations. The expression 'personal protection' refers to the bodyguarding of senior members of staff who run the risk of abduction or even assassination. VIP protection is big business for specialist companies which, in the main, are staffed by former Special Forces operatives, former policemen and intelligence officers.

Surveillance here refers *not* to the use of electronic gadgets but to the *in situ* watching and following of individuals. 'Tailing' as it is sometimes called is a security skill that requires certain expertise and knowledge. A skilful operative is capable of following a person by vehicle or foot anywhere, anytime, in any circumstances.

Required Skills

All surveillance operatives should have the following skills:

Expert driving of cars and motorcycles.

Being adept at personal disguise.

The ability to talk one's way out of unusual situations when challenged by members of the public or police.

Enough patience to go long periods of time without refreshment or toilet facilities. **NB:** It is not unusual for surveillance operations to extend twenty hours, or even longer.

No matter what area (geographically) a surveillance operation is located, the '*Watchers*' should be familiar with the general lay of the land.

Even those possessing the above mentioned skills, will come unstuck if they do not also have considerable 'on-the-job' experience. It is true to say that there are hundreds of very professional and capable criminal and security investigators in the private and official sector who have no experience of surveillance, and who would not be able to conduct even a simple 'watching' operation. '*Watching*' is a specialist skill.

Surveillance Operations

Motor Vehicle Tracing

An important consideration in all surveillance operations is motor vehicle registration numbers. Such information is a useful method of tracking an unidentified person to an address; it is therefore essential that those engaged in this kind of work get into the habit of noting car registration numbers of any vehicle that appears to be associated with the subject of investigation. For those who have a requirement to seek the name and address of drivers, the following information will be of assistance.

The location of the office issuing any particular UK car registration is determined by the letters accompanying the index number of a vehicle. The majority of vehicle registrations have a group of two or three letters together – where there are *two*, these signify the issuing office and where there are *three* letters, the last two refer to the identity of the issuing authority. By cross-referencing with the list below, the likely origin of the car's registration can be divined.

MOTOR VEHICLE REGISTRATION LETTERS

AA	Bournemouth		CB	Manchester
AB	Worcester		CC	Bangor
AC	Coventry		CD	Brighton
AD	Gloucester		CE	Peterborough
AE	Bristol		CF	Reading
AF	Truro		CG	Bournemouth
AG	Hull		CH	Nottingham
AH	Norwich		CJ	Gloucester
AJ	Middlesbrough		CK	Preston
AK	Sheffield		CL	Norwich
AL	Nottingham		CM	Liverpool
AM	Swindon		CN	Newcastle-upon-Tyne
AN	Reading		CO	Exeter
AO	Carlisle		CP	Huddersfield
AP	Brighton		CR	Portsmouth
AR	Chelmsford		CS	Glasgow
AS	Inverness		CT	Lincoln
AT	Hull		CU	Newcastle-upon-Tyne
AU	Nottingham		CV	Truro
AV	Peterborough		CW	Preston
AW	Shrewsbury		CX	Huddersfield
AX	Cardiff		CY	Swansea
AY	Leicester			
			DA	Birmingham
BA	Manchester		DB	Manchester
BB	Newcastle-upon-Tyne		DC	Middlesbrough
BC	Leicester		DD	Gloucester
BD	Northampton		DE	Haverfordwest
BE	Lincoln		DF	Gloucester
BF	Stoke-on-Trent		DG	Gloucester
BG	Liverpool		DH	Dudley
BH	Luton		DJ	Liverpool
BJ	Ipswich		DK	Manchester
BK	Portsmouth		DL	Portsmouth
BL	Reading		DM	Chester
BM	Luton		DN	Leeds
BN	Manchester		DO	Lincoln
BO	Cardiff		DP	Reading
BP	Portsmouth		DR	Exeter
BT	Newcastle		DS	Glasgow
BS	Aberdeen		DT	Sheffield
BT	Leeds		DU	Coventry
BU	Manchester		DV	Exeter
BV	Preston		DW	Cardiff
BW	Oxford		DX	Ipswich
BX	Haverfordwest		DY	Brighton
BY	London NW			
			EA	Dudley
CA	Chester		EB	Peterborough

EC	Preston	GH	London SW
ED	Liverpool	GJ	London SW
EE	Lincoln	GK	London SW
EF	Middlesbrough	GL	Truro
EG	Peterborough	GM	Reading
EH	Stoke-on-Trent	GN	London SW
EJ	Haverfordwest	GO	London SW
EK	Liverpool	GP	London SW
EL	Bournemouth	GR	Durham
EM	Liverpool	GS	Luton
EN	Manchester	GT	London SW
EO	Preston	GU	London SE
EP	Swansea	GV	Ipswich
ER	Peterborough	GW	London SE
ES	Dundee	GX	London SE
ET	Sheffield	GY	London SE
EU	Bristol		
EV	Chelmsford	HA	Dudley
EW	Peterborough	HB	Cardiff
EX	Norwich	HC	Brighton
EY	Bangor	HD	Huddersfield
		HE	Sheffield
FA	Stoke-on-Trent	HF	Liverpool
FB	Bristol	HG	Preston
FC	Oxford	HH	Carlisle
FD	Dudley	HJ	Chelmsford
FE	Lincoln	HK	Chelmsford
FF	Bangor	HL	Sheffield
FG	Brighton	HM	London C
FH	Gloucester	HN	Middlesbrough
FJ	Exeter	HO	Bournemouth
FK	Dudley	HP	Coventry
FL	Peterborough	HR	Swindon
FM	Chester	HS	Glasgow
FN	Maidstone	HT	Bristol
FO	Gloucester	HU	Bristol
FP	Leicester	HV	London C
FR	Preston	HW	Bristol
FS	Edinburgh	HX	London C
FT	Newcastle-upon-Tyne	HY	Bristol
FU	Lincoln		
FV	Preston	IA–IZ	See last page in the Section
FW	Lincoln		
FX	Bournemouth	JA	Manchester
FY	Liverpool	JB	Reading
		JC	Bangor
GA	Glasgow	JD	London C
GB	Glasgow	JE	Peterborough
GC	London SW	JF	Leicester
GD	Glasgow	JG	Maidstone
GE	Glasgow	JH	Reading
GF	London SW	JJ	Maidstone
GG	Glasgow	JK	Brighton

JL	Lincoln	LR	London NW
JM	Reading	LS	Edinburgh
JN	Chelmsford	LT	London NW
JO	Oxford	LU	London NW
JP	Liverpool	LV	Liverpool
JR	Newcastle-upon-Tyne	LW	London NW
JS	Inverness	LX	London NW
JT	Bournemouth	LY	London NW
JU	Leicester		
JV	Lincoln	MA	Chester
JW	Birmingham	MB	Chester
JX	Huddersfield	MC	London NE
JY	Plymouth	MD	London NE
		ME	London NE
KA	Liverpool	MF	London NE
KB	Liverpool	MG	London NE
KL	Liverpool	MH	London NE
KD	Liverpool	MJ	Luton
KE	Maidstone	MK	London NE
KF	Liverpool	ML	London NE
KG	Cardiff	MM	London NE
KH	Hull	MN	(Not used)
KJ	Maidstone	MO	Reading
KK	Maidstone	MP	London NE
KL	Maidstone	MR	Swindon
KM	Maidstone	MS	Edinburgh
KN	Maidstone	MT	London NE
KO	Maidstone	MU	London NE
KP	Maidstone	MV	London SE
KR	Maidstone	MW	Swindon
KS	Edinburgh	MX	London SE
KT	Maidstone	MY	London SE
KU	Sheffield		
KY	Coventry	NA	Manchester
KW	Sheffield	NB	Manchester
KX	Luton	NC	Manchester
KY	Sheffield	ND	Manchester
		NE	Manchester
LA	London NW	NF	Manchester
LB	London NW	NG	Norwich
LC	London NW	NH	Northampton
LD	London NW	NJ	Brighton
LE	London NW	NK	Luton
LF	London NW	NL	Newcastle-upon-Tyne
LG	Chester	NM	Luton
LH	Bournemouth	NN	Nottingham
LJ	Bournemouth	NO	Chelmsford
LK	London NW	NP	Worcester
LL	London NW	NR	Leicester
LM	London NW	NS	Glasgow
LN	London NW	NT	Shrewsbury
LO	London NW	NU	Nottingham
LP	London NW	NV	Northampton

NW	Leeds	QY	
NX	Dudley	RA	Nottingham
NY	Cardiff	RB	Nottingham
		RC	Nottingham
OA	Birmingham	RD	Reading
OB	Birmingham	RE	Stoke-on-Trent
OC	Birmingham	RF	Stoke-on-Trent
OD	Exeter	RG	Newcastle-upon-Tyne
OE	Birmingham	RH	Hull
OF	Birmingham	RJ	Manchester
OG	Birmingham	RK	London NW
OH	Birmingham	RL	Truro
OJ	Birmingham	RM	Carlisle
OK	Birmingham	RN	Preston
OL	Birmingham	RO	Luton
OM	Birmingham	RP	Northampton
ON	Birmingham	R	Nottingham
OO	Chelmsford	RS	Aberdeen
OP	Birmingham	RT	Ipswich
OR	Portsmouth	RU	Bournemouth
OS	Glasgow	RV	Portsmouth
OT	Portsmouth	RW	Coventry
OU	Bristol	RX	Reading
OV	Birmingham	RY	Leicester
OW	Portsmouth		
OX	Birmingham	SA	Aberdeen
OY	London NW	SB	Glasgow
		SC	Edinburgh
PA	Guildford	SD	Glasgow
PB	Guildford	SE	Aberdeen
PC	Guildford	SF	Edinburgh
PD	Guildford	SG	Edinburgh
PE	Guildford	SH	Edinburgh
PF	Guildford	SJ	Glasgow
PG	Guildford	SK	Inverness
PH	Guildford	SL	Dundee
PJ	Guildford	SM	Carlisle
PK	Guildford	SN	Dundee
PL	Guildford	SO	Aberdeen
PM	Guildford	SP	Dundee
PN	Brighton	SR	Dundee
PO	Portsmouth	SS	Aberdeen
PP	Bournemouth	ST	Inverness
PR	Luton	SU	Glasgow
PS	Bournemouth	SV	Spare
PT	Durham	SW	Dumfries
PU	Chelmsford	SX	Edinburgh
PV	Ipswich	SV	See below *
PW	Norwich	SY	See below *
PX	Portsmouth		
PY	Middlesbrough	TA	Exeter
		TB	Liverpool
QA–	London C	TC	Bristol

TD	Manchester	VJ	Gloucester
TE	Manchester	VK	Newcastle-upon-Tyne
TF	Reading	VL	Lincoln
TG	Cardiff	VM	Manchester
TH	Swansea	VN	Middlesbrough
TJ	Liverpool	VO	Nottingham
TK	Exeter	VP	Birmingham
TL	Lincoln	VR	Manchester
TM	Luton	VS	Luton
TN	Newcastle-upon-Tyne	VT	Stoke-on-Trent
TO	Nottingham	VU	Manchester
TP	Portsmouth	VV	Northampton
TR	Portsmouth	VW	Chelmsford
TS	Dundee	VX	Chelmsford
TT	Exeter	VY	Leeds
TU	Chester		
TV	Nottingham	WA	Sheffield
TW	Chelmsford	WB	Sheffield
TX	Cardiff	WC	Chelmsford
TY	Newcastle-upon-Tyne	WD	Dudley
		WE	Sheffield
UA	Leeds	WF	Sheffield
UB	Leeds	WG	Sheffield
UC	London C	WH	Manchester
UD	Oxford	WJ	Sheffield
UE	Dudley	WK	Coventry
UF	Brighton	WL	Oxford
UG	Leeds	WM	Liverpool
UH	Cardiff	WN	Swansea
UJ	Shrewsbury	WO	Cardiff
UK	Birmingham	WP	Worcester
UL	London C	WR	Leeds
UM	Leeds	WS	Bristol
UN	Exeter	WT	Leeds
UO	Exeter	WU	Leeds
UP	Newcastle	WV	Brighton
UR	Luton	WW	Leeds
US	Glasgow	WX	Leeds
UT	Leicester	WY	Leeds
UU	London C		
UV	London C	X	Northumberland CC
UW	London C	XA	Greater London C & Kirkaldy DC
UX	Shrewsbury	XB	Greater London C Monklands DC
UY	Worcester		(Coatbridge)
		XC	Greater London C & MC Solihull
VA	Peterborough	XD	Greater London C & B of Luton
VB	Maidstone	XE	Greater London C & B of Luton
VC	Coventry	XF	Greater London C & B of Torbay
VD	Luton (Series withdrawn)	XG	Middlesbrough BC
VE	Peterborough	XH	Greater London C
VF	Norwich	XI	Central Office, Coleraine
VG	Norwich	XJ	Manchester City
VH	Huddersfield	XK	Greater London C

XL	Greater London C
XM	Greater London CO
XN	Greater London CO
XO	Greater London C
XP	Greater London C
XR	Greater London C
XS	Renfrew DC (Paisley)
XT	Greater London C
XU	Greater London C
XV	Greater London C
XW	Greater London C
XX	Greater London C
XY	Greater London C
XZ	Central Office, Coleraine

Note	*The **XA-XY** series has not been issued since October 1974*

YA	Taunton
YB	Taunton
YC	Taunton
YD	Taunton
YE	London C
YF	London C
YG	Leeds
YH	London C
YJ	Brighton
YK	London C
YL	London C
YM	London C
YN	London C
YO	London C
YP	London C
YR	London C
YS	Glasgow
YT	London C
YU	London C
YV	London C
YW	London C
YX	London C
YY	London C

ZA	Dublin
ZB	Cork
ZC	Dublin
ZD	Dublin
ZE	Dublin
ZF	Cork
ZG	Dublin
ZH	Dublin
ZI	Dublin
ZJ	Dublin
ZK	Cork

ZL	Dublin
ZM	Galway
ZN	Meath
ZO	Dublin
ZP	Donegal
ZR	Wexford
ZT	Cork
ZU	Dublin
ZW	Kildare
ZX	Kerry
ZY	Louth
ZZ	Temporary registration

AZ	Belfast
BZ	Down
CZ	Belfast
DZ	Antrim
EZ	Belfast
FZ	Belfast
GZ	Belfast
HZ	Tyrone
JZ	Down
KZ	Antrim
LZ	Armagh
MZ	Belfast
NZ	Londonderry
OZ	Belfast
PZ	Belfast
RZ	Antrim
SZ	Down
TZ	Belfast
UZ	Belfast
VZ	Tyrone
WZ	Belfast
XZ	Armagh
YX	Londonderry
ZZ	Dublin (temporary)
IA	Ballymena
IB	Armagh
IC	Carlow
ID	Cavan
IE	Clare
IF	Cork
IH	Donegal
IJ	Downpatrick
IK	Dublin
IL	Enniskillen
IM	Galway
IN	Kerry
IO	Kildare
IP	Kilkenny
IR	Offaly
IT	Leitrim

IU	Limerick	LI	Westmeath
IW	Londonderry	MI	Wexford
IX	Longford	NI	Wicklow
IY	Louth	OI	Belfast
IZ	Mayo	PI	Cork
		RI	Dublin
AI	Meath	TI	Limerick
BI	Monaghan	UI	Londonderry
CI	Laois	WI	Waterford
DI	Roscommon	XI	Belfast
EI	Sligo	YI	Dublin
FI	Tipperary (N. Riding)		
HI	Tipperary (S. Riding)		
JI	Armargh		
KI	Waterford		

*The SV and SY marks are allocated to all LVLO's for issue to vehicles which require a non-suffix mark on registration

For example, a vehicle showing the registration K343 LAD, will have been issued by *Gloucester* licensing office. The identification of the Registered Keeper of any UK registered vehicle may be obtained from DVLC, Swansea. Applications may only be made in writing and a suitable reason for the request must be stated.

Other identifying features of a car or motorcycle registration that can lead to the name and address of the driver can be found in small print at the bottom of a licence plate; this information identifies the name and telephone number of the garage supplying the vehicle on the occasion it was initially taxed and registered. In the case of recent registrations, it is highly likely that the garage named will have the identity of the person who purchased the vehicle, along with details of any finance or hire purchase firm involved. All the enquirer has to do is to extract the information from the garage sales department.

Another useful method of tracking the driver to his home address is the already briefly mentioned Hire Purchase Information (HPI) service. This unique organisation is located in Salisbury and was formed in 1938. The company was founded to combat multiple financing fraud on automobiles. Over 50 years later, HPI uses the latest information and computer technology to provide a vital fraud prevention service to a wide range of subscribers, including local and national government bodies.

HPI's databases contain over 65 million records across eight on-line registers. This wealth of information is held on powerful fault-tolerant dual-sited Tandem computer systems. Several million assets, mainly private and commercial motor vehicles, plus 22 other categories of mobile assets, are registered with this firm. The operations division in Salisbury handles over 53,000 enquiries a day. All information registered relates to motor vehicles of one kind or another, and HPI also operates a link to the Driving Licence Centre at Swansea for the purpose of carrying out car registration checks, which is the service of primary interest to individuals engaged in surveillance or special investigations which involve cars. Also held on HPI records are details of hire purchase or other loan agreements. Enquirers are able to confirm the details of such loans, including the name and telephone number of the bank or finance loan company, from where it should be possible, with the co-operation of the firm, to track down the user of a particular vehicle.

It should be appreciated that the HPI service is only available to registered subscribers of Hire Purchase Information PLC. Also, it would be unlawful to persuade a serving police officer or other government official to obtain motor vehicle registration details. All methods of obtaining names and addresses of motor vehicles must be conducted in a legal and proper manner.

Surveillance Tactics

Preparation   Before mounting a surveillance operation, certain pre-tailing procedures should be adopted. First, suitable operatives must be briefed and discreet vehicles prepared; ideally, motorcycles should be used. Conspicuous cars would *not* be appropriate, and all operatives, some of whom should be female, must be discreetly and casually dressed so that a quick change of external clothing is possible. Wherever possible, photographs of the subject would be helpful; in any event, prior to commencement a detailed description of the subject, along with the type and registration number of any vehicle associated with them, should be available.

No matter what the reason or the degree of importance for a 'watching' investigation, it would not be wise for only one person to be engaged on such work. The chances of success will be minimal, and the possibility of a driving accident when following increases three-fold on such occasions.

The recommended minimum number of watchers is four, split between two vehicles, which ideally would be a motorcycle plus a non-descript car or van. It is important that all operatives have a communications facility in the form of body-worn transmitters, ear-pieces, and discreet throat or miniature hand microphones. Large, hand-held 'walkie-talkie' equipment should be avoided. Any vehicle used must also be fitted with communications equipment that can be operated from the vehicle's battery, thus avoiding a drain on the personal, less powerful equipment. Obviously, within reason, the more operatives the better.

Communications equipment   All equipment used in security work should be legally licensed in accordance with current legislation. This is an important requirement, for the simple reason that all speech transmitted over the airwaves will be heard by someone else. If it transpires such communications are in fact illegal then the surveillance team could be interfering with a vital services frequency. It is therefore very important that the choice and use of communications equipment is made with specialist advice, and only after the appropriate authority has granted permission for its use.

An Example Tailing Operation

The following extract from a surveillance report compiled by Eurotec investigators in respect of an industrial espionage case, serves as a good example of what can be experienced during a watching operation. There are various potentially 'inconvenient' situations waiting to arise, and the ingenuity of the operatives has to be such that those problems do not affect the operation.

A private surveillance team comprising four operatives, divided between a motorcycle and a car, kept watch on an office manager of a computer firm based near Heathrow Airport. The object of the exercise was to confirm the movements of the Suspect on a specific day. There was a radio communications link between all four operatives, who are referred to as *Echo Tango* one, two, three and four.

At 5am, Echo Tango 1 and 2 arrived at the Subject's Beaconsfield address and set up an observation point a short distance from the premises. Both operatives were concealed in the rear of a transit van, the remaining operatives were located out of sight of the address with a motorcycle which was to be the primary 'tailing' method throughout the day. Echo Tango 4 was to be the pillion rider, and in addition to being responsible for videoing the Subject's movements she was also expected to act as a general safety observer for the driver of the motorcycle. In the event the Subject took to foot, Echo Tango 4 would be expected to leave the motorcycle pillion to follow.

The observation point on this occasion was most inconvenient, in that the house was situated in a cul-de-sac. Fortunately, most of the residents in the road lived in large houses, which meant that their private motor vehicles were kept in garages. This left plenty of room for the positioning of a surveillance van (which is not always the case). Whilst this was in some respects convenient for operatives, it did in fact result in the van looking rather out of place, so much so that an elderly male walking a dog appeared to get suspicious at the sight of the vehicle. Fortunately, his dog decided to take off after a cat and the old man was distracted from the vehicle and its occupants.

Between 5am and 7.30am there was very little movement at the address, apart from the delivery of milk and mail. Nothing occurred at the address until 7.40am, when the Subject left, driving a BMW vehicle which had been kept out of sight of the road in a double garage attached to the house.

Immediately on sighting the Subject, Echo Tango 1 called the motorcycle team, relaying the description and registration number of the BMW. A few moments later, Echo Tango 3 confirmed that contact had been made with the Subject and that they were in pursuit. For a period of twenty-five minutes the motorcycle team followed the BMW, which took them to another private address in Slough where the Subject entered the house with his own key. It later transpired that this was in fact the home of his parents where he had called in for a visit.

Adhering to normal procedure, Echo Tango 3 had provided regular position reports to the transit van, which had made its way to the Slough address, arriving at approximately 8.10am. By now, two magnetic signs advertising a building firm had been attached to the side of the vehicle. Once in place, the transit took over the job of watching the Slough address and once again the motorcycle kept out of sight.

At 9am the Subject was again on the move; by this time traffic conditions were so heavy that Echo Tango 3 was obliged to keep very close to the BMW. However, this did not create any real problem as there were a number of motorcycles on the road at the same time. The transit, guided by the motorcycle team, gradually made its way in the general direction taken by the Subject of investigation, which was towards the Post House Hotel, West Drayton, Middlesex.

At 9.25am the BMW arrived at the car park of the Post House, and the driver entered the building. Echo Tango 4 left the motorcycle and, after quickly dispensing with her crash helmet and anorak, followed the Subject into the reception area, where she observed him talking to a middle aged man and woman. After managing to covertly video the group, she took up a vantage point from where she could see and hear what was being discussed.

While Echo Tango 4 was maintaining watch within the reception/lounge area of the Post House, the transit van was making its way to the car park, where it arrived at approximately 10.00am. Within seconds of arriving, the builders' signs were changed in favour of florist's signs. Throughout the morning, Echo Tango 4 alternated with Echo Tango 1 and 2, and between them they managed to monitor the movements and conversations of the Subject and his associates, who at 11.30am were joined by two younger males.

At 12.30pm, the group entered the Carvery Restaurant where they remained deep in conversation until 2.45pm. With a little ingenuity, Echo Tango 2 and 4 managed to acquire a table adjacent to the group, from where all conversations were tape recorded.

After taking coffee in the reception area, the group dispersed and the primary Suspect walked to his BMW car where he sat talking into a cellular telephone for 15 minutes. The remainder of the group walked to a Ford Granada vehicle, the registration number of which was recorded by one of the surveillance team. This information was to play an important part in subsequent investigations.

After terminating his cellular telephone conversation, the Subject of investigation drove out of the car park, and proceeded to the town centre of Windsor, where he arrived at 4.30pm. By now the surveillance team had been joined by an additional pair of operatives who, using a saloon car, took over from the transit van. The female pillion passenger taking to the streets to follow the Suspect on foot, while the saloon car and motorcycle waited in the area of a multi-story car park in which the BMW had been parked. For thirty minutes the female operative gave a running commentary on the movements of the BMW driver, who thereafter returned to his car and drove off towards his home in Beaconsfield; this time the saloon car and motorcycle alternated the following between them.

NB: It is important, when undertaking mobile surveillance, for a following vehicle or motorcycle to attempt to use other traffic as a shield from the target of investigation. There are occasions, however, when traffic conditions are such that it will be necessary to take up a position directly behind the Suspect; when approaching traffic lights for example.

On occasions when two or more vehicles are being used on the surveillance, then 'tailing' from in front as well as behind is one useful method of following in heavy traffic. In any event, during all surveillance operations, whenever money will allow, three or four vehicles (cars, vans and motorcycles) should be used. This will enable the watchers to alternate vehicles throughout the operation. In very heavy, slow-moving traffic, for example in towns and cities, it would also be wise to keep a push bike in one of the cars or vans.

Foot surveillance   To start with at least four operatives should be used. Women are particularly useful for such work, and at least two would be useful in the team. When undertaking foot surveillance, all operatives on the ground should be in radio contact with each other. Ideally, ear-pieces and throat microphones connected to concealed transmitters would be more suitable than hand-held 'walkie-talkies'. A press-to-talk switch can also be held inside a pocket, or in the palm of the hand.

In the above example, Eurotec was greatly inhibited by the client's reluctance to incur the cost of any more operatives than the two vehicles and four agents. When the Suspect took to foot in Windsor, the use of one agent, for what was nothing more than a visit to local shops, was considered the best method of operation.

Throughout foot surveillances it is imperative that one operative acts as a team leader, controlling the whole of the operation. It will be his or her job to ensure that no one operative remains close to, or in sight of the target for long periods of time. This is achieved by rotating all those involved at regular intervals to different positions in front of and behind the Suspect.

Static Surveillance

This kind of observation work is not only boring, but fraught with potential compromise; this is why more unscrupulous operators resort to illegal forms of electronic bugging to collect evidence on an individual's activities. Someone has to be available for long periods of time to watch a domestic or business address. This means that some kind of observation post has to be set up, which invariably involves a vehicle being present in the neighbourhood for some considerable time. Neighbours' attention is likely to be attracted and a complaint made to the local police, who would be obliged to investigate.

Liaising with police   It is important (and sensible) for all static surveillance operations to be brought to the notice of local police. A simple courtesy visit to the local station nearest to the target, is all that is required. This does not mean that the police have to be informed in any great detail of the reasons for the surveillance. In fact only the identity of the firm carrying out the work and a general reason need to be given. It would also be helpful to police if the registration number of vehicles responsible for the operation were provided; the police would then have it on record that strangers are in their area and a lawful investigation is taking place.

If a member of the public made a complaint they would simply be reassured that there was nothing to worry about.

Liaising with a police force or any other official agency, including the security services, does not require those engaged in a private investigation to impart confidential details of such activity. Such officials should only be entrusted with what they need to know.

Pre-surveillance checks Before engaging in any form of static observation, a visit should be made to the address and a *reconnaisance* carried out. The general lie of the land should be noted and the courtesy visit made to the local police station. Once familiarisation with the area has been completed, then a suitable vantage point for the observation vehicle should be chosen.

The best type of vehicle to use for this kind of work would be a discreet, one-way windowed van. Operatives should be able to secret themselves in the rear and have some kind of security window through which they can observe and film events as they occur. Contact with base is also important, and can be conveniently achieved with cellular phones, or radio walkie-talkies.

In security operations where a static *and* mobile surveillance is being conducted, then mobile members of the team should be kept out of sight of the address and only contacted by radio as and when they are required. Under no circumstances should the static observation vehicle ever be opened-up to other members of the team, members of the public, or even for that matter to a police officer who could well appear on the scene to investigate the vehicle's presence in the area. If a police officer or member of the public starts to show an interest in the static observation post, then a radio call should be made to a nearby mobile member of the team who can deal with the matter.

Personal Protection

Protecting VIP's is probably the biggest money-earner for private security firms in the UK. It is not a job for the untrained and inexperienced, and this kind of work should always be passed to specialists.

It is a sad fact of business life that there are numerous business-men and women who are at risk of being abducted or even murdered. Organised criminal gangs and terrorists are quick to identify a high-profile target and how much can be made from a kidnapping. To make matters worse, insurance companies are now offering 'hostage insurance' that guarantees to pay a ransom in the event of an abduction. In other words, kidnappers cannot fail to collect. Former Special Forces soldiers have formed bodyguard organisations that are earning hundreds of thousands of pounds a year protecting businessmen and women. This kind of protection work is so much in demand, that most security firms and detective agencies offer such services.

Most high-profile industrialists are at risk. In fact, anyone who is a valuable and senior member of a rich industrial or commercial firm is a potential kidnap victim. One particular London security firm earns in excess of two million pounds a year protecting clients. This organisation, which is operated by former Scotland Yard officers, Military Intelligence agents and Special Air Service soldiers, has been responsible for the protection of numerous household names in the UK. On one occasion when a client was abducted and held to ransom by the IRA, this firm actually engaged in hostage negotiations with the terrorists. Their brief was to secure the release of the client by bartering over the amount of ransom the insurance company were prepared to pay out.

Organising protection for VIP business persons is complicated work that should only be entrusted to professionals. Having said that, potential targets can (and should) adopt various common-sense precautions that will contribute to their safety.

Safety Checklist

1. Always be observant when on the move.
2. Instruct secretaries and telephone staff *not* to acknowledge your movements and whereabouts to strangers.
3. Do not accept telephone calls without first of all confirming the identity of the caller.
4. When carrying out regular journeys, always vary the route.
5. When travelling by road, alone or accompanied, always keep the doors of the vehicle locked.
6. Wherever possible, maintain contact with office and home.
7. Refrain from discussing on the telephone confidential information relating to your whereabouts and movements.
8. Under no circumstances agree to appointments with strangers. Always obtain evidence of their identity and address.
9. Ensure that all written documents relating to personal movements and activity are confidential to just those who need to know.
10. Do not leave personal diaries or appointment books lying around.

Protecting High-risk Persons

Business persons requiring personal protection should expect their general way of life to change from the offset of sharing their lives with bodyguards. Any potential hostage must realise that if there is in fact a risk then 24-hour protection is going to be necessary: work, home, holidays, weekends will all be shared with their escorts. It is important that all individuals employed as bodyguards are of a similar type and presentation as the people in the environment they are employed. Escorts should be dressed in civilian clothing, similar to the 'principal' (the person under protection) also, the intellectual standard should wherever possible be on a par with the client and their associates.

In cases where the client is of a high risk, a minimum of a four-handed team should be employed on a round-the-clock basis. The team should be comprised of a team leader, two assistant operatives and a relief operative.

The job of the team leader is to organise and control the whole escort operation. Whatever he or she says should be obeyed without question. Invariably, such people are highly experienced in VIP protection and are able to sense when situations are not right and about to change. In addition to being in charge, the team leader is also an active member of the squad throughout the tour of duty. The two assistants are also fully operational, whereas the relief member of the team is not fully active as such, but is on standby for occasions when other operatives require to visit the toilet or break for refreshments.

At all times at least one member of the team should be present with the principal, and the remaining two close at hand, acting as a shield or barrier. For example, if the client is engaged in normal business activity, then one operative will be present in the office with him and the remaining members outside the door keeping watch. The relief person could be in a nearby rest-room or office, relaxing. In all personal security operations, team members should be in constant contact with each other via a secure radio network and, if required, be able to reach the principal within seconds.

Client in transit   There will be many occasions when the client will be mobile, either on foot or in some form of public or private transport. The team leader (who should be in possession of comprehensive details of the principal's movements) will be able to advise his colleagues accordingly and ensure the following checks are carried-out before travel is commenced.

(a)   The principal's car is checked, and the driver ready to move off as soon as the group arrive.

(b)   The area surrounding the vehicle is safe.

(c)   The driver is aware of the destination and route to be taken. It is important that the driver is given adequate notice of all journeys planned by the principal.

(d)   Any escort vehicle should also be checked for safety and serviceability, and the driver suitably informed.

(e)   Drivers of the principal's car, and any escort vehicle, should be carefully selected and trained in high speed and evasive driving. Furthermore, whenever possible such individuals should be an additional but integral part of the security team protecting the principal. This being the case, drivers will come under the control of the team leader.

(f)   In cases where the client is able to afford and has sanctioned the use of security guards in excess of the recommended minimum-four, it would be useful to engage a further two operatives with an additional vehicle. Their expertise could be utilised as an advanced observation party. By travelling ahead of the main vehicle and escort, a check could be carried out of the route to anticipate any planned kidnap attempt.

(g)   On occasions when the principal is static inside an office or other premises, the additional members of the team can be used to maintain observation in the surrounding external area.

Use of weapons and force   Private security officers in the UK are not legally entitled to carry weapons of any kind. Furthermore, excess use of force will almost certainly lead to a prosecution of any security person. This legal restraint means that those engaged in VIP protection have to rely on common-sense planning, along with their powers of observation, if they are to avoid kidnap situations. In the event the client is in fact attacked, then physical fitness and experience in unarmed combat might be of value in any confrontation.

In the event an attempt is made to abduct the client the team members closest to the principal should adopt whatever course of action they consider necessary to protect their charge. Simultaneously, a pre-selected member of the team, who is in possession of an electronic attack bleeper device should activate the emergency button. This will in turn transmit a recorded security message to a central control area, from where information of the attack will be relayed on to police headquarters. These automatic emergency bleepers are very useful aids, and are essential tools of the trade for personal protection officers. In addition to transmitting a pre-recorded message, they also act as 'locater' beacons.

Defence of the principal   In any unarmed combat situation, the defender is at an obvious disadvantage if the abductors are armed. Criminals have a vast array of weaponry at their disposal and it would not be unusual for bodyguards to find themselves surrounded by kidnappers armed with powerful automatic weapons.

Despite the weakness of their situation, bodyguards can put up a reasonable show of resistance. To start with, they do have access to a very powerful weapon of their own – the principal's motor vehicle. Immediately an attack is detected, the driver of the principal's car should adopt the following procedures.

(1) Confirm the car doors are locked.
(2) Activate his own emergency bleeper, which should also be programmed into a central security control.
(3) By using the car as a weapon, the driver should then forcibly drive away from the area, crashing through any vehicles blocking the way. By skilful driving, forward and reversing as required, it should be possible to thwart the abductors.

Members of the team who find themselves engaged in hand to hand combat (assuming it is their choice to resist) should make every attempt to take possession of any firearms being used by the attackers. If this is achieved then, depending on the progress of the attack and in particular the amount of violence that can legally be used to protect the principal and the team members, it might be wise to consider using any captured weapon in self-defence. It must be said however, that according to law one can only use *the minimum amount of force necessary*.

When disarming an attacker, a bodyguard (who no doubt would be familiar with and capable of using a firearm) should remember that there is an obligation that has to be exercised in respect of *members of the public*. To take possession of an automatic weapon is one thing, but to start firing it on the streets of a major city could well lead to the shooting of an innocent person.

Non Resistance

There are any number of advocates of 'no resistance' when it is known that a kidnap attempt is underway. According to such experts, there is little point in risking life and limb when all the abductors are after is money. Presumably, what these people are inferring is that to simply pay up is the better course of action to take. Whilst this might seem to be the most convenient method of dealing with an abduction, there are unforeseen circumstances that could develop. There is nothing worse than having to negotiate with a passionate political terrorist whose beliefs and requirements have nothing to do with money. Such a person requires very little provocation to put a bullet into the head of a hostage.

At the end of the day, the decision to enter into unarmed combat with the enemy is down to the individual team members. Individually, they must decide whether or not to risk their lives for their fat cat client. In the main, security persons engaged on VIP protection duties are former Special Forces and Military Intelligence personnel.

Post Kidnapping Procedures

Should it transpire that the principal is in fact successfully kidnapped, then the following procedures should be adopted.

(1) Return to base and set up a control centre manned by trained security hostage negotiators.
(2) Tape recorders should be installed on all telephone lines.
(3) Impose a complete news blackout; interference from the press will only inhibit a successful recovery.
(4) Inform the police.

It will not be a long wait before the first telephone call is received, demanding either money or courses of action to be activated. However, before entering into any dialogue with the kidnappers, proof of the principal's condition should be requested.

Negotiation The period of negotiation will be a tense and difficult time for all concerned. Police involvement will restrict the victim's own security staff from getting involved too deeply, and of course if the client is insured, assessors and negotiators from the company providing cover will almost certainly become involved.

In return for the client's safe release, it will be worthwhile allowing the insurance negotiators a free hand. Such individuals have good relations with the authorities, and some are former intelligence officers who have access to unusual sources that can be very beneficial in a kidnap situation. So much so that in the past it has been known for private negotiations to secure the release of victims who were able to pay up either privately or with insurance.

Negotiation is a delicate and difficult task which should only be carried out by experts. The client's security staff can contribute to the whole recovery operation by maintaining good relationships with the authorities, and under no circumstances should any course of action that might upset negotiations be attempted.

Private training courses   There are a number of private courses available to suitable individuals having a requirement for such training. Any businessman who would like to submit company staff for instruction in VIP protection can apply to any one of a number of firms, such as C.Q.B. Services, Tactical Training International in Liverpool.

This organisation is staffed by former Special Forces soldiers and other close-quarter battle experts, and between them provide training in most aspects of VIP close protection. C.Q.B. Services enjoys world wide connections and hosts regular courses and seminars, often attended by famous security experts.

In addition to the above organisation there are other less military-oriented training courses organised by schools where one can learn the art of **evasive driving**, which is an important skill for the private bodyguard. Details of such firms are included in the reference section.

9   Legal Procedures and Intelligence Services

A major contribution to business failure against the background of economic slowdown, is the fact that many companies have been driven to employ the services of expensive lawyers and accountants to deal with situations that could have been easily avoided or dealt with in-house. This tendency to run to one's solicitor in the hope of rectifying a business problem is an unwise course of action to take; especially if the solicitor is one of the many that have recently been accused of milking clients and other crooked deals.

One just has to read the glut of recent exposés of the legal profession revealing all manner of illegality – from stealing clients' money, to overcharging, and even defrauding building societies and banks – to realise that employing a member of the legal profession can be quite hazardous and dangerous to business health.

The most recent report of this kind appeared in the *Daily Mail* on 23 February 1995, when Whitehall Correspondent Steve Doughty revealed that a vast spiral of fraud and abuse was robbing the Legal Aid system of millions of pounds. This investigation centred around crooked lawyers who, according to a scathing report by the Auditor General, Sir John Bourn, had been responsible for trickery which had left the taxpayers with bills for consultations and advice that was either not needed or not given. According to the report, there was also evidence of solicitors pre-dating application forms for Legal Aid, forging signatures and exaggerating the amount of time worked on a case.

From the general contents of this report and the comments of the Lord Chancellor, Lord Mackay, it would appear that members of the illustrious British legal system have for some considerable time, on a wide scale, been fleecing the Legal Aid system out of millions of pounds a year. If this then is the case, what chance has anyone in business when in the hands of a solicitor? Even honest lawyers are expensive and furthermore, when barristers become involved the costs are going to be horrendous.

Avoiding Expensive Legal Advice

Whilst it is obviously more economical to avoid expensive lawyers whenever possible, there will be occasions when it might well be prudent to be represented by a solicitor. If and when such an occasion presents itself, to request **written confirmation** of the solicitor's charges would be a sensible course of action in the first instance.

It is surprising just how many businessmen instruct solicitors without realising what it will cost them. And when they receive a bill for several thousands of pounds for what they thought was a simple matter, they are unable to comprehend how such expense is justified.

The lawyer-client relationship should be such that at all times the client is fully informed as to the various stages a case has reached, and what the costs are at any given point in time. It is also important to remember that the client is responsible for instructing the solicitor what courses of action should be activated. This can only be achieved if the client is fully informed and aware of what is going on and the courses of action open to him.

In today's business climate, more and more company directors and managers are adopting a 'DIY approach' to situations that in the past have normally been passed to solicitors. For example, collecting evidence from witnesses in statement form, does not require the expensive services of a solicitor.

Interviewing a Witness

Anyone who finds themselves in a situation that requires the evidence of a witness to be given to another, especially in a legal dispute that could end up in court, is well advised to arrange for the witness to be interviewed and a signed statement obtained.

The art of interviewing requires patience and the ability to transform what a witness says into a clear, concise written account of what occurred. Under no circumstances should the witness be led, or suggestions made as to what happened. It would be sensible and productive to arrange for the interviewer to be someone who was not involved in the dispute or problem being discussed.

From the start of the interview a rapport should be created with the interviewee, who should be allowed refreshments and the most comfortable surroundings for the discussion. Before formally writing the statement down, it would be advisable to seek the witness's cooperation in providing the required evidence. Even if a witness is unwilling to give evidence, they can in fact be ordered to attend a court for the purpose of revealing what they know about a specific incident or subject.

Format and content of statements Witness statements should resemble verbal evidence as far as possible. It is not admissible to include hearsay or opinion evidence in a statement. County Court regulations relating to format and content of statements differ slightly from evidence produced in criminal cases. According to County Court Rules Order 20, Rule 12a, a statement should include:

1. The witness's full name, residence; or if a witness in a business capacity, the place of work, employer or firm and the position, occupation and relationship to the matter discussed.
2. Language of the statement should as far as possible be that of the witness and not of the interviewer. When lawyers take witness statements, they have a habit of legalising or intellectualising the expressions of the witness. This is not necessary.
3. The statement should follow the chronological sequence of events and be divided into numbered paragraphs, each dealing with a distinct part of the evidence.

STATEMENT OF: *John Smith*
ADDRESS: *234 Grosvenor Way*
                          London W18 9LP
TELEPHONE: *0181-345-6789*

WILL SAY: I am a bookkeeper employed by GM Enterprises
Limited, of Wellock Industrial Estate, Slough. I have been
employed in this capacity for 12 years.

1.   On 1 January 1995 I was working in the accounts department.
Shortly after 2pm a man dressed in a blue windcheater walked into
the office and said to me that he had been asked by my boss to
collect the electric typewriter for servicing. I pointed to the desk
where the machine was and told him that was the only electric
machine we had so that it must be the one.

2.   He walked over to the desk, unplugged it and walked out of
the office with it under his arm. That was the last I saw of the
machine and the man. I understand that it has in fact gone
missing and that Mr Jackson, my boss, had not in fact authorised
any servicing on any office machinery.

3.   On 12 February 1995 at 1pm I was in the area of Park Lane,
London, when I saw a man I recognised as the same person who
had taken our typewriter. He was entering a small office machinery shop called 'Office Machines'. I checked the number on the
door and saw that it was located at number 56 Park Lane. I looked
inside the door and saw the man standing behind the counter, he
appeared to be serving a customer.

SIGNED: *John Smith*
WITNESSED BY: *D Jones*
DATED: *2/2/95*

STATEMENT OF WITNESS
(C.J. Act 1967 s.9; M.C. Act, 1980, s.102; M.C. Rules 1981 r.70)

Statement of (name of witness) _____

Age of Witness (& date of birth) _____

Occupation of Witness _____

Telephone No. _____

Address _____

_____

_____ Post Code _____

Telephone Number _____

Taken by :   Date :   Time :

_____
_____
_____
_____
_____
_____
_____
_____
_____
_____
_____
_____
_____
_____
_____
_____
_____
_____
_____
_____
_____
_____
_____
_____
_____

(Signed)

This statement (consisting of .... pages each signed by me) is true to the best of my knowledge and belief and I make it knowing that, if it is tendered in evidence, I shall be liable to prosecution if I have wilfully stated in it anything which I know to be false or do not believe to be true.

Dated the   day of   19 (Signed) ....

4. The statement should be typed double spaced on one side of the paper only.
5. The statement must be dated.
6. The statement must be signed by the witness.
7. The statement must contain an assurance that the contents are true to the best of the witness's knowledge and belief.
8. The statement must identify any document or item mentioned in evidence.

All statements can initially be recorded in handwriting by the interviewer, who will produce a typed version for further signature at a later date (see p 144). It would be prudent to tape-record any interview with a witness. This can be done with or without the witness's agreement.

In cases where the evidence of a witness is likely to be required in a *Criminal Court*, then the slightly different format would be advisable (see p 145).

Attending Court to Give Evidence

Many witnesses dread having to attend a court of law for the purpose of giving evidence. Although this should not be a worrying occasion, the pompous and at times insulting attitude of those questioning people from ordinary walks of life can be quite an experience for the faint-hearted. The following checklist might assist those expecting to have to attend a court of law for the purpose of giving evidence.

Witness Checklist

1. All evidence is given on oath, this means swearing (on the Holy Bible) to tell the truth.
2. Witnesses are normally questioned by either barristers, solicitors, registrars or judges, depending on what kind of court is dealing with a case.
3. After taking the oath, remain calm and wait until questions are asked.
4. Do not allow the questioner to confuse you, remain calm and simply tell what you believe to be the truth.

5. Address all answers to the jury (if such a trial) or to the judge or registrar. Do not feel obliged to answer directly to a barrister or lawyer. The jury, judge or registrar are responsible for reaching a verdict, and these are the people who will be impressed (or unimpressed) with the evidence presented.

6. In the event a ruthless questioner attempts to confuse or trick a witness, the best advice one can give is to remain calm and politely request clarification of the question. If irrelevant questions are put to a witness, the judge or registrar can be asked if this irrelevancy has to be addressed.

7. It is important to remember that a witness must not feel threatened to such an extent they end up agreeing to words that have been put into their mouths by smooth-talking barristers or solicitors, who are the biggest worry when giving evidence. The truth means very little to such people: *winning* is the primary goal, and the truth sadly remains in the background. This is not so when being examined by a registrar or judge, who are independent of opposing camps.

Access to Official Data

There are numerous occasions in business when there is a legal requirement for official information. Regrettably, in the United Kingdom there is an obsession for withholding most kinds of information. Many people are unable to comprehend why criminal records information is withheld from those who have a genuine requirement to have access to such data. Even reputable firms who find themselves being fleeced by members of staff who are rumoured to have a criminal record cannot rely on any official assistance.

This situation has resulted in a proliferation of organisations providing a number of highly illegal services. Nothing is secure from these individuals, who in the main are from private detective agencies and security firms.

Not only is criminal records data freely available on the open market, it is also possible to illegally acquire information held by the Ministry of Defence, the DSS, Special Branch and security services, Customs and Immigration, British Telecom, Cellular

Telephone, banks and other finance houses, and local councils.

These examples are the tip of an iceberg which is currently being investigated by officers from Scotland Yard's Complaints Investigation Bureau, who have unearthed a nationwide system operated by security firms, private detectives, solicitors and public organisations who have been dealing in stolen official data.

While many businessmen may consider it acceptable to pay for stolen official information, it should be remembered that to do so is a serious criminal offence and could result in a breach of the **Official Secrets Act**. Furthermore, depending on the circumstances of such an offence, and in particular who was involved, a more serious offence of conspiracy or even corruption could apply.

A newly-introduced law makes it illegal to acquire in any way, data stored in a computer that is registered with the **Data Protection Registrar**. This new legislation is yet another step to increase the restrictions that are already in place. Whether or not this will result in the cessation of illegal accessing by security firms and detective agencies is anyone's guess. Be that as it may, as long as business proprietors and directors realise the various ramifications of buying official data, they can act accordingly.

Government Intelligence Services

It is important for all businesses to be aware that it is not uncommon for British and foreign spy organisations to overtly request the assistance of suitable firms or solo businessmen (and women). As readers will no doubt recall, the recent well-publicised Scott enquiry has highlighted the use of British firms by the secret intelligence service (MI6).

Whilst some may consider it appropriate to allow their firm to be used as an intelligence cover, and directors and/or proprietors may feel inclined to act as informers for MI5 or the American CIA, they should be advised that all kind of compromising situations can, and have been known to, ensnare willing helpers. It is not the purpose of this book to elaborate on this kind of work conducted by the numerous spy organisations, except to point out the potential dangers of getting involved.

There are two kinds of approaches one should be aware of. Whatever method is used, one should never forget that deception is the intelligence service's trade.

Overt method   This is a simple, open approach by a representative of the department concerned who makes only a little secret of who he/she represents. It is then usual for a straightforward request to be put to the targeted business. In an attempt to ensure collaboration, the spy will invariably home-in on the target's patriotism, if that fails then mercenary 'carrots' will be offered. If the business person approached is not agreeable, then any skeletons that have been uncovered will be used to lean on the target. Blatant blackmail is not uncommon – threats of exposure of criminal offences and promises of contracts are the norm in such situations.

Covert method   This is much more difficult to detect, in that the approach is never actually spelt out in chapter and verse. The intelligence operative usually approaches the target in some kind of business capacity, generally as a client who pays for a specific service. A relationship develops with the new 'client', and before long the target is ensnared into providing a service of value to the intelligence organisation. In some cases the supplier may not have any idea what is going on. Another covert method often adopted is for spies to obtain employment with private firms, providing themselves with a cover for their clandestine activities.

Before knowingly agreeing to tendering any assistance to an Intelligence organisation, consult the following checklist.

Checklist

1.   Ask to see identification.
2.   Covertly tape record all discussions.
3.   Obtain a formal written description of what is required.
4.   Ensure that an authentic full address is supplied.
5.   If contemplating getting involved, then introduce a third party as a witness, preferably a solicitor who can advise on the various legal aspects of such work.

6. Do not sign any Official Secrets Act documents.
7. Do not be seen in any public place with an intelligence agent. To be exposed as an informer could compromise in any number of ways; especially in cases where arms or drugs are involved.

Having pointed out the negative aspects of relationships with Intelligence or other government departments, it is also true to say that such relationships can in some cases be quite straightforward and uncompromising, providing formal written agreements are exchanged.

Private companies trading abroad are regularly monitored by MI6 to see if any use can be made of their contact with foreign countries. MI5 on the other hand concentrate on home-based firms, who might from time to time be of use in counter-intelligence work. Police, and other law enforcement agencies also rely from time to time on private firms for specific assistance or 'cover'.

Useful Addresses and Information

Police, Military and General Security Information

Metropolitan Police
New Scotland Yard,
Broadway,
London SW1H 0BG
Tel: 0171 230 1212

City of London Police
26 Old Jewry,
London EC2R 8DJ
Tel: 0171 601 2222

Avon & Somerset Constabulary
P.O. Box No. 37,
Portishead,
Bristol BS20 8QJ
Tel: 01275 818181

Bedfordshire Police
Woburn Road,
Kempstone,
Bedford MK43 9AX
Tel: 01234 841212

Cambridgeshire Constabulary
Hinchingbrooke Park,
Huntingdon PE18 8NP
Tel: 01480 456111

Cheshire Constabulary
Castle Esplanade,
Chester CH1 2PP
Tel: 01244 350000

Cleveland Constabulary
P.O. Box No. 70,
Ladgate Lane,
Middlesbrough,
Cleveland TS8 9EH
Tel: 01642 326326

Cumbria Constabulary
Carleton Hall,
Penrith,
Cumbria CA10 2AU
Tel: 01768 891999

Derbyshire Constabulary
Butterley Hall,
Ripley,
Derbyshire DE5 3RS
Tel: 01773 570100

Devon & Cornwall Constabulary
Middlemoor,
Exeter EX2 7HQ
Tel: 01392 52101

Dorset Police
Winfrith,
Dorchester,
Dorset DT2 8DZ
Tel: 01929 462727

Durham Constabulary
Aykley Heads,
Durham DH1 5TT
Tel: 0191 386 4929

Dyfed-Powys Police
P.O. Box No. 99,
Llangunnor,
Carmarthen SA31 2PF
Tel: 01267 236444/7

Essex Police
P.O. Box No. 2,
Springfield,
Chelmsford,
Essex CM2 6DA
Tel: 01245 491491

Gloucestershire Constabulary
Holland House,
Lansdown Road,
Cheltenham,
Glos. GL51 6QH
Tel: 01242 521321

Greater Manchester Police
P.O. Box 22 (S. West PDO),
Chester House,
Boyer Street,
Manchester M16 0RE
Tel: 0161 872 5050

Gwent Constabulary
Croesyceiliog,
Cwmbran,
Gwent NP44 2XJ
Tel: 01633 838111

Hampshire Constabulary
West Hill,
Winchester,
Hants. SO22 5DB
Tel: 01962 868133

Hertfordshire Constabulary
Stanborough Road,
Welwyn Garden City,
Herts. SL8 6XF
Tel: 01707 331177

Humberside Police
Queens Gardens,
Kingston-upon-Hull,
Humberside HU1 3DJ
Tel: 01482 26111

Kent County Constabulary
Sutton Road,
Maidstone,
Kent ME15 9BZ
Tel: 01622 690690

Lancashire Constabulary
P.O. Box No. 77,
Hutton,
Nr. Preston,
Lancs. PR4 5SB
Tel: 01772 614444

Leicestershire Constabulary
P.O. Box No. 999,
Leicester LE99 1AZ
Tel: 01533 530066

Merseyside Police
P.O. Box 59,
Liverpool L69 1JD
Tel: 0151 709 6010

Northamptonshire Police
Wootton Hall,
Northampton NN4 0JQ
Tel: 01604 700700

North Wales Police
Glan-y-Don,
Colwyn Bay LL29 8AW
Tel: 01492 517171

Nottingham Constabulary
Sherwood Lodge,
Arnold,
Nottingham NG5 8PP
Tel: 01602 670999

South Yorkshire Police
Snig Hill,
Sheffield S3 8LY
Tel: 01742 768522

Suffolk Constabulary
Martlesham Heath,
Ipswich IP5 7QS
Tel: 01473 613500

Sussex Police
Malling House,
Lewes,
Sussex BN7 2DZ
Tel: 01273 475432

Lincolnshire Police
P.O. Box No. 999,
Lincoln LN5 7PH
Tel: 01522 532222

Norfolk Constabulary
Martineau Lane,
Norwich NR1 2DJ
Tel: 01603 768769

Northumbria Police
Ponteland,
Newcastle-upon-Tyne NE20 0BL
Tel: 01661 872555

North Yorkshire Police
Newby Wiske Hall,
Northallerton,
North Yorkshire DL7 9HA
Tel: 01609 783131

South Wales Constabulary
Bridgend CF31 3SU
Tel: 01656 655555

Staffordshire Police
Cannock Road,
Stafford ST17 0QG
Tel: 01785 57717

Surrey Police
Mount Browne,
Sandy Lane,
Guildford,
Surrey U3 1HG
Tel: 01483 571212/9

Thames Valley Police
Kidlington,
Oxon OX5 2NX
Tel: 01865 846000

Warwickshire Constabulary
P.O. Box No. 4,
Leek Wootton,
Warwick CV35 7QB
Tel: 01926 415000

West Mercia Constabulary
Hindlip Hall,
Hindlip
P.O. Box No. 55,
Worcester WR3 8SP
Tel: 01905 723000

West Midlands Police
P.O. Box No. 52,
Lloyds House,
Colmore Circus,
Queensway,
Birmingham B4 6NQ
Tel: 0121 626 5000

West Yorkshire Police
P.O. Box No. 9,
Wakefield,
West Yorkshire WF1 3QP
Tel: 01924 375222

Wiltshire Constabulary
London Road,
Devizes,
Wiltshire SN10 2DN
Tel: 01380 722341

Ministry of Defence Police
Headquarters, Empress State Building, Lillie Road, London SW6 1TR
Tel: 0171 824 444

The Ministry of Defence Police is a statutory civil police force with a particular responsibility for the security and policing of the MoD environment. It provides and contributes to the physical protection of property and personnel within its jurisdiction and provides a comprehensive police service to the MoD as a whole.

Royal Naval Regulating Branch
Provost Marshal (Royal Navy), Office of Naval Home Command,
Portsmouth PO1 3LR
Tel: 01705 822351 Ext. 23195

The Regulating Branch is the Service Police of the Royal Navy. Apart from an administrative and security role in ships and naval establishments there are a number of Royal Navy Provost headquarters in the United Kingdom whose role may be summarised as follows:

1. *The provision of a Service Police facility in major naval ports, each complemented with Unit Investigators.*
2. *In Portsmouth the provision of a Special Investigation Branch which includes a drugs dogs detachment.*

Royal Military Police

Provost Marshal (Army), Bray House, Worth Down, Winchester SO21 2RG
Tel: 01962 887370

The Royal Military Police is the Army's police force whose role of policing the Army at home and overseas in peace and war may be summarised as follows:

(a) The provision of garrison police facilities.

(b) Law enforcement and crime prevention; and liaison with Home Office and other police forces worldwide when the Army interests are involved or suspected.

(c) Tactical military police support to the Army in all places of military operations.

(d) The provision of Close Protection worldwide to those deemed by MoD to warrant such.

Royal Air Force Police

Ministry of Defence (Air) Directorate of Security & Provost Marshall (RAF)
Room 5258, Main Building, Whitehall, London SW1A 2HB
Tel: 0171 218 3998

The RAF Police are responsible for criminal investigations, counter-terrorism and counter-intelligence activities and general police matters that affect the Royal Air Force. They are established at most RAF stations in the United Kingdom and abroad. Investigations are the responsibility of Headquarters Provost and Security Services (UK) which functionally controls its subordinate units. The RAF Police School is responsible for all RAF Police and RAF Police dog training, whilst the Provost and Security Liaison Officer provides specialist advice at the RAF Personnel Management Centre.

Atomic Energy Authority Constabulary

Building E6, AEA Technology, Culham Laboratory, Abingdon,
Oxfordshire OX14 3DB

The Constabulary is employed to police AEA Technology and British Nuclear Fuels plc establishments in the United Kingdom.

British Transport Police

P.O. Box No. 260, 15 Tavistock Place, London WC1H 9SJ
Tel: 0171 388 7541

The British Transport Police is the national police for the railways, policing British Rail and London Underground, whilst serving the whole community.

Department of Transport – Transport Security Division
Room S8/09, Dept. of Transport, 2 Marsham Street, London SW1P 3EB

The Department of Transport, through the National Aviation Security Programme, requires United Kingdom airports, British airlines worldwide and foreign airlines operating in the United Kingdom to take measures to protect airports, airlines and air navigation installations against acts of violence. Aviation Security Inspectors are authorised by the Secretary of State under the Aviation Security Act 1982, as amended by the Aviation and Maritime Security Act 1990, to inspect and test the measures taken by these bodies.

Department of Transport – Air Accidents Investigation Branch
DRA, Farnborough, Hampshire GU14 6TD
Tel: 01252 510300

Civil Aviation Authority
Investigation Branch, Room No. T1323, CAA House, 45–59 Kingsway, London WC2B 6TE
Tel: 0171 379 7311 Ext. 5325

H.M. Customs and Excise Invesigation Division
Custom House, Lower Thames Street, London EC3R 6EG
Tel: 0171 283 5353

Post Office Investigation Department
Impact House, 2 Edridge Road, Croydon CR9 1PJ
Tel: 0181 681 9259

The POID deals with, or assists police, etc in dealing with, criminal offences affecting the Post Office and the Department of National Savings. It also provides a crime prevention advisory service for these businesses.

BT Security and Investigation Directorate
Sunrise Parkway, Linford Wood, Milton Keynes MK14 6PH
Tel: 01908 693939 (General Enquiries),
0171 356 500 (Out of hours for all urgent BT enquiries)

BT Investigation and Detection Unit is responsible for dealing with or assisting police with all criminal matters affecting BT.

Mercury Communications Ltd
26 Red Lion Square, London WC1R 4HQ
Tel: 0171 528 2000

The Mercury Corporate Risk Department is responsible for the physical security of the network, crime prevention, security surveys, protection of information and the investigation of criminal and security matters in conjunction with appropriate police, security and government departments.

HMSO – Security Control Office
Britannia House, 7 Trinity Street, London SE1 1DA
Tel: 0171 378 6741

The office authenticates all security documents produced by HMSO on behalf of government departments, government agencies and other customers. Counterfeit documents are identified, expert witness statements provided and court attended as required. This office is responsible for all criminal matters affecting documents produced by HMSO.

Ministry of Agriculture Fisheries and Food Investigation Branch
55 Whitehall, London SW1A 2EY
Tel: 0171 270 8364

Intervention Board
Anti-Fraud Unit Headquarters, Fountain House, 2 Queen's Walk,
P.O. Box No. 69, Reading, Berkshire RG1 7QW
Tel: 01734 583626

The Anti-Fraud Unit is responsible for investigating fraud against the Common Agricultural Policy in the United Kingdom. The Unit is based in Reading and its 8 investigators cover the UK working in conjunction with HM Customs and Excise, the appropriate police forces and MAFF.

Department of Employment (Employment Service) BMB2
Level 3 Rockingham House, 123 West Street, Sheffield S1 4ER
Tel: 01742 596334

This section investigates benefit fraud against the Employment Service and liaises with police and other investigation agencies. Its activities are nationwide, linked through benefit fraud units in provincial centres.

Department of Social Security Benefits Agency – Organised Fraud Units
Block 2, Spur T North, Government Buildings, Honeypot Lane, Stanmore,
Middlesex HA7 1AY

Departments of Trade and Industry Investigations Division
Ashdown House, 123 Victoria Street, London SW1E 6RB

Main powers of the division are to examine on a confidential basis the records of a company, under section 447 of the Companies Act 1985. The investigation of the affairs or ownership of a company under sections 431, 432 or 442 of the Companies Act 1985, or of allegations of inside dealing under section 177 of the Financial Services Act 1986. The prosecution of various offences including those associated with insolvencies. Seeks in the public interest, the winding up of the companies and the disqualification of offenders from acting as company directors.

Board of Inland Revenue Investigation Office
Angel Court, 199 Borough High Street, London SE1 1HZ
Tel: 0171 234 3884

Officers of the Board's Investigation Office undertake the majority of Criminal Investigations on behalf of the Inland Revenue.

British Broadcasting Corporation Investigator's Office
BBC, White City, 201 Wood Lane, London W12 7TS
Tel: 0181 752 4168

One of the functions of the Investigators is to liaise with the police in all matters relating to BBC Radio and Television. Their services are readily available to police officers requiring assistance or information.

Radio Investigation Service
Waterloo Bridge House, Waterloo Road, London SE1 8UA
Tel: 0171 215 2062

The RIS enforces the Wireless Telegraphy Acts and associated legislation and acts against illegal users of radio. The service is able to assist the police in tracing illegal radio communications.

Charity Commission Monitoring and Investigation Division
St Alban's House, 57–60 Haymarket, London SW1Y 4QX
Tel: 0171 210 4477

Under section 8 of the Charities Act 1993, Monitoring and Investigation Staff are empowered to investigate and check abuse within the charity sector.

Tobacco Advisory Council
Glen House, Stag Place, London SW1E 5AG
Tel: 0171 834 7085

The Tobacco Advisory Council have an office whose principal objectives are: (i) to develop close and effective links and act as a main point of contact for the police, the Home Office, H.M. Customs, National Transport Agencies and other appropriate organisation in all matters relating to the prevention and detection of crime affecting tobacco goods; and (ii) to collaborate with the responsible representatives of tobacco manufacturers and importers in the United Kingdom in improving and co-ordination of security systems aimed at protecting manufactured tobacco from theft and fraud. Its services are readily available to police officers requiring information and assistance.

Wine & Spirit Security Liaison Ltd
346 Kennington Road, London SE11 4LD
Tel: 0171 735 6255

The aims and objectives of this company, which represents the majority of UK Distillers and Producers of gin, whisky, vodka etc and importers of fine wines and brandy are (i) to promote and foster means to improve the safety of members goods in any part of the UK, Republic of Ireland, Isle of Man, Channel Islands and Europe, whether in transit or in store, depots, warehouses etc, (ii) to maintain close liaison with police forces, H.M. Customs and Excise, the Home Office, insurance and transport agencies etc to prevent loss by hijacking and other criminal acts including fraud and (iii) render all possible assistance to the appropriate authorities whenever necessary.

VISA – Visa International Services Association
P.O. Box No. 253, London W8 5TE (Visa Service Centre)
Tel: 0171 937 1179

The Visa Service Centre's telephone number was introduced in 1986 specifically as a contact point for law enforcement assistance. All collect calls are accepted. Whilst the VSC Operators are restricted in the type of information they are permitted to release on Visa Cards and Travellers Cheques they can provide contact information on Visa Member Banks worldwide 24 hours a day every day of the year.

Jockey Club Security Department
42 Portman Square, London W1H 0EN
Tel: 0171 935 9251/0969

To provide all the services necessary to co-ordinate, control, administer and supervise all aspects of security and security forces at racecourses. To prevent or minimise horse doping, crime and other improper practices connected with horse racing and to co-operate with the local police forces as necessary to achieve these objectives. To collect information and statistics relevant to the above tasks and circulate information thereon to the appropriate authorities.

Public Offices, Associations and Professional Bodies

Association of British Chambers of Commerce
9 Tufton Street,
London SW1P 3QB

Association of British Investigators
ABI House, 10 Bonner Hill Road,
Kingston-upon-Thames,
Surrey

Asssociation of Law Costs Draftsman
16 Langley Way,
West Wickham,
Kent BR4 0DP

Association of Legal Secretaries
The Mill,
Clymping Street,
Clymping,
Littlehampton,
West Sussex BN17 5RN

Association of Professional Computer Consultants
109 Baker Street,
London W1M 2BH

Attorney General's Chambers, Law Officers' Department
Royal Courts of Justice,
Strand,
London WC2A 2LL

Audit Office, National
157–197 Buckingham Palace Road,
Victoria,
London SW1M 9SP

Bankruptcy, High Court of Justice in
Thomas More Building,
Royal Courts of Justice,
Strand,
London WC2A 2LL

Central Office of Information
Hercules Road,
Westminster,
London SE1 7DU

Companies House
Companies House holds the public records of more than a million companies. It provides a range of services to make it easier to access information and file documents. Details can be obtained from the Cardiff address.

Birmingham
Central Library,
Chamberlain Square,
Birmingham B3 3HQ
Tel: 0121 233 9047

Cardiff
Crown Way,
Cardiff CF4 3UZ
Tel: 01222 388588,
Central Enquiries Tel: 0122 380801

Edinburgh
100–102 George Street,
Edinburgh EH2 3DJ
Tel: 0131 255 5774

Glasgow
108 Bothwell Street,
Glasgow G2 7JP
Tel: 0141 248 3315

Leeds
25 Queen Street,
Leeds LS1 2TW
Tel: 01532 338338

London
55–71 City Road,
London EC1Y 1BB
Tel: 0171 253 9393

Manchester
75 Mosley Street,
Manchester M2 2HR
Tel: 0161 236 7500

**Crown Agents for Overseas
   Governments and
   Administrations**
St. Nicholas House,
St Nicholas Road,
Sutton,
Surrey SM1 1EL

**Foreign and Commonwealth
   Office**
King Charles Street,
London SW1A 2AH

**General Register Office
   (Population/Census)**
St. Catherine's House,
10 Kingsway, London WC2B 6JP

Home Office
50 Queen Anne's Gate,
London SW1H 9AT

Institute of Directors
116 Pall Mall,
London SW1Y 5ED

**Institute of Management
   Consultants**
32–33 Hatton Garden,
London EC1N 8DL

**Institute of Professional
   Investigators**
31a Wellington Street,
St. Johns,
Blackburn BB1 8AF

**Land Registry, H.M.
   (Headquarters)**
32 Lincoln's Inn Fields,
London EC2A 3PH

Law Society
113 Chancery Lane,
London WC2A 1PL

Lloyd's of London
1 Lime Street,
London EC3M 7DQ

Lloyd's Register of Shipping
71 Fenchurch Street,
London EC3M 4BS

**Lord Chancellor's Office
  Headquarters**
26–28 Old Queen Street,
London SW1H 9HP

**National Pharmaceutical
  Association Ltd**
Mallinson House,
40–42 St. Peter's Street,
St. Albans,
Herts AL1 3NP

Northern Ireland Office
Old Admiralty Building,
Whitehall,
London SW1A 2AZ
and Stormont Castle,
Belfast WC1B 3QH

Office of Fair Trading
Field House,
15–25 Bream's Buildings,
London EC4A 1PR

Official Receiver (London)
21 Bloomsbury Street,
London WC1B 3QH

Passport Office
Clive House,
70–78 Petty France,
London SW1H 9HD

Public Record Office
Ruskin Avenue,
Kew, Richmond,
Surrey TW9 4DU
(modern department records)
Chancery Lane,
London WC2R 1LR
(legal and medieval records)

**The Registry of County Court
  Judgements**
173–5 Cleveland Street,
London W1P 5PE

Scottish Office
Dover House,
Whitehall,
London SW1A 2AU
and New St. Andrew's House,
St. James's Centre,
Edinburgh EH1 3TB

Stationery Office, H.M.
Government Bookshop,
49 High Holborn,
London WC1V 6HB

**VAT Central Unit (Customs
  and Excise)**
Alexander House,
21 Victoria Avenue,
Southend-on-Sea,
Essex SS99 1AA

Investigation, Security and Credit Reference Agencies

The Association of British Investigators
ABI House,
10 Bonner Hill Road,
Kingston-upon-Thames,
Surrey KT1 3EP
0181 546 3368

Nationwide members
experienced in most
aspects of criminal and
security investigations

Eurotec (Investigators & Consultants)
27a Old Gloucester Street,
London WC1N 3XX
0171 404 5011

Established in 1968 and
experienced in all types
of investigations,
counter-intelligence and
personal security.

The Malthouse
Runnymede Road,
Egham,
Surrey TW20 9BO
01784 434712

Nationwide service and
members of the A.B.I.

CCN Credit Systems
Talbot House,
Talbot Street,
Nottingham NG1 5HF
01602 410888

General credit checking
and on-line computer
services. Company
searches and County
Court Judgement
information.

Equifax Europe (UK) Ltd
Coombe Cross,
2/4 South End,
Croydon CR0 1DL
0181 680 8295

Credit checking, voters
lists and County Court
Judgement searches on
telephone or on-line
computer service.

HP Information
Dolphin House,
PO Box 61,
New Street,
Salisbury,
Wilts. SP1 2TB
01722 413434

Motor vehicle ownership
checks. Is linked to the
DVLC Swansea.

Phonetic Alphabet

In order to avoid confusion caused by like-sounding letters when using radio or telephone communications, an internationally recognised system of words for letters is used. These are shown below.

A	ALPHA	N	NOVEMBER
B	BRAVO	O	OSCAR
C	CHARLIE	P	PAPA
D	DELTA	Q	QUEBEC
E	ECHO	R	ROMEO
F	FOXTROT	S	SIERRA
G	GOLF	T	TANGO
H	HOTEL	U	UNIFORM
I	INDIA	V	VICTOR
J	JULIET	W	WHISKEY
K	KILO	X	X-RAY
L	LIMA	Y	YANKEE
M	MIKE	Z	ZEBRA

References

Eurotec (Investigators & Consultants)

Association of British Investigators (ABI)

Lord Chancellor's Department

Guildford County Court

How to collect money owed to you by Mel Lewis published by McGraw-Hill Book Co. Ltd.

How to understand and use company accounts by Roy Warren published by Hutchinson Business Books

Police & Constabulary Almanac (1994) published by R Hazell & Co.

Index by John Preece published by Protecall, Birmingham

Index